Scientific Misconduct and Its Cover-Up

Diary of a Whistleblower

Solomon Rivlin, Ph.D.

BrownWalker Press
Boca Raton · 2004

Scientific Misconduct and Its Cover-Up:
Diary of a Whistleblower

Copyright © 2004 Solomon Rivlin

BrownWalker Press
Boca Raton, Florida
USA · 2004

ISBN: 1-58112-422-8

BrownWalker.com

Preface

The events and personalities described in the following account are real. Names and places were changed to protect the identity of the people who took part in this ugly drama, one that unfortunately, is duplicated in other academic institutions in the United States and elsewhere. By protecting the identity of the innocent and that of the whistleblower I am, regrettably, also protecting the identity of the guilty.

With the scarcity of research funds ever more acute, many other cases of misconduct in science are bound to occur. Since the majority of the research funds in the US are awarded to universities and research institutes by the government of the United States of America, the American public must be assured that its tax money does not fund research fraud. Whether or not the public will be privy to these cases depends, to a large extent, on the honesty, integrity and openness of the people conducting the investigations of cases of scientific misconduct. Similar to the church's long and relentless efforts to obscure cases of sexual abuse, many academic institutions have chosen to cover up their own cases of scientific misconduct. People within these institutions involved in these cover-ups should be held responsible for wrongdoing as much as those who commit the specific cases of scientific misconduct.

Another hurdle preventing full exposure of such cases is the high risk faced by whistleblowers everywhere. These courageous people routinely pay an extremely high price for daring to reveal wrongdoing in science and academe. It is unfortunate that most whistleblowers are standing alone against much greater forces in the institutions where fraud occurs. They cannot count on open support from their colleagues who fear retaliation and retributions. Although both federal and state laws exist that aim at protecting the whistleblower, only 30 states do have such laws. Both federal and state laws are weak, offering limited protection for the whistleblower. Many who blow the whistle still pay dearly for their actions and in cases where the law intervenes on behalf of the whistleblower this intervention mostly comes too late.

Neither scientists nor the public should blindly accept the claims of several people within the scientific community that cases of scientific misconduct are rare. No one really knows how many misconduct cases exist, since often they remain unreported or covered up by the very people in charge of investigating and exposing them and punishing the perpetrators.

The events described in this book are the account of one such case of scientific misconduct and its cover-up. It is hoped that this account will make scientists, faculty members and students everywhere more aware of their duty to expose scientific misconduct, on one hand, and be aware of the inherent risks and pitfalls of becoming a whistleblower in science, on the other.

Table of Contents

Cast of Characters (in order of appearance)

Wendy S. Capegoat – The lab director of the Chairman of the Neuroscience Department at the Medical School, Jefferson University, Jefferson City, KS. Unbeknown to her she became the scapegoat for the misdeeds of her boss.

Dr. Lidia Quarry – Associate Professor, Neuroscience Department, Jefferson University Medical School, Jefferson City, KS; an outstanding young neuroscientist who was recruited by her chairman for her knowledge and experience in the field of Alzheimer's disease research, only to be robbed of them by the person who recruited her.

Dr. Frank I. M. Moral – Chairman of the Neuroscience Department, Jefferson University Medical School, Jefferson City, KS, had a unique way to come up with research ideas and how to fund them.

Jeremy M. Artyr – A doctoral student at the Neuroscience Department, Jefferson University Medical School, Jefferson City, KS, who worked under the mentorship of three scientists. He found out that one of his mentors had claimed ownership of his intellectual property.

Dr. Christian C. Heat – Vice Chairman and later Chairman of the Neurology Department, Jefferson University Medical School, Jefferson City, KS, a physician who would do anything to assure his advancement, including scientific misconduct.

Dr. George O. M. Budsman – Ombudsman, Jefferson University Medical School, Jefferson City, KS, who, despite his many years at this position had never dealt with a case of scientific misconduct until…

Dr. Dean A. Verage – Dean (1982–1999), Jefferson University Medical School, Jefferson City, KS, a pathologist who was elected as the dean because of his mediocrity.

Dr. Harvey L. Powerhouse – Chairman (1976–1997), Neurology Department, Jefferson University Medical School, Jefferson City, KS, who willed great influence over the future of Dean Verage and the future of his vice chair, Dr. Christian C. Heat.

Dr. Donald V. Icedean – Vice Dean for Academic Affairs, Jefferson University Medical School, Jefferson City, KS, an academician-turned-administrator who forgot his academic roots.

1

Dr. Bertha I. Clash – Associate Dean for Research, Jefferson University Medical School, Jefferson City, KS, has been an associate in Dr. Moral's Neuroscience Department. She gladly accepted her dean's assignment despite a clear conflict of interest.

Dr. Simon Wall – Professor, Anesthesiology Department, Jefferson University Medical School, Jefferson City, KS. A research scientist who discovered a whole new facet of science he was not aware existed.

Dr. David O.K. Yesmam – Associate Provost, Jefferson University, Jefferson City, KS, a "yes man" of his attractive female boss.

Dr. Barry A. L. Truist – Chairman (1982–2000), Anesthesiology Department, Jefferson University Medical School, Jefferson City, KS, a gentle, caring man, a great educator and an exemplar for young physicians and who strongly believes in the goodness of mankind.

Dr. James V. Shepherd – President (1996–2003), Jefferson University, Jefferson City, KS, an academician and an excellent communicator who had brought to his position, what had seemed to be, a new and healthy spirit.

Dr. Caroline X. Pretty – Provost, Jefferson University, Jefferson City, KS, an attractive woman who cared more about her looks than her job as the highest academic officer at the university. In early 2003 she was selected as the President of Arkansas University. Eventually, she continued to work with Dr. Shepherd on some extracurricular issues.

Myron R. E. Porter – The science reporter for *The Jefferson City Times*, who was informed about a case of scientific misconduct at the university and through the "Freedom of Information Act", managed to receive much of the information about the case directly from the university administration.

Dr. Nina Marshal – Vice president for Research, Jefferson University, Jefferson City, KS, a biologist par excellence who was lured to become a top administrator and left her lab bench for good.

Dr. Michael A. Walton – A junior physician, Director, Princeton Institute for Infectious Disease Research, Medicine Department, Jefferson University Medical School, Jefferson City, KS, who became another instrument in the hands of the administration in their retaliatory battle against the whistleblower.

Dr. Ming U. Meek – Professor, Neuroscience Department, Jefferson University Medical School, Jefferson City, KS, a meek and gentle researcher whom Dr. Moral loved to harass.

Dr. David S. Neaky – A candidate for a faculty position at the Neuroscience Department, Jefferson University Medical School, Jefferson City, KS, who played a crucial role in complicating things for the whistleblower.

Dr. Jonathan S. Nobb – Dean of the Medical School, Jefferson University, Jefferson City, KS, who replaced the retiring dean, Dr. Verage, in July, 1999, and gladly took over the campaign that intended to teach the whistleblower a lesson.

Allan U. Griever – Chairman, Faculty Grievance Committee, Medical School, Jefferson University, Jefferson City, KS.

Dr. Keath H. Wright – Professor, Neuroscience Department, Jefferson University Medical School, Jefferson City, KS, a long-time colleague and friend of Simon Wall, an honest, straight forward, no frills man and an extremely bright scientist. One of the three mentors of Jeremy M. Artyr.

Dr. Stewart P. Retender – Vice Chairman, Neuroscience Department, Jefferson University Medical School, Jefferson City, KS, a pompous anatomist who did not hesitate to bend the rules for his own personal benefits and who led a grievance campaign against the whistleblower.

Julie L. Swim – Assistant Program Director of the American Society of Neuroscientists.

Nora Burgen – Executive Director of the American Society of Neuroscientists.

James F. Edwin – President of the American Society of Neuroscientists, 1999–2000.

Dr. Lola I. Serve – Professor, Neuroscience Department and Associate Dean for Faculty Affairs, Jefferson University Medical School, Jefferson City, KS, a neuroscientist in Dr. Frank I.M. Moral's department who has become an administrator. She saw nothing wrong in ignoring her own conflict of interests in the service of her masters.

Dr. Gary A. Goodwill – Associate Professor, Bacteriology Department, Jefferson University Medical School, Jefferson City, KS, the only faculty member in the Medical School who was willing, openly, to support and encourage the whistleblower throughout his ordeal.

Dr. Tina Chancey – Professor, Pharmacology Department, Jefferson University Medical School, Jefferson City, KS, member, Faculty Grievance Committee.

Cornelia Shaw – Assistant to the Dean of the Medical School, Jefferson University, Jefferson City, KS.

Dr. Carla L. Pool – Chairperson (2000- present), Anesthesiology department, Jefferson University Medical School, Jefferson City, KS, a personal friend of the dean, Dr. Nobb, who forced her candidacy for the chair position of the department against the will of its faculty members.

Dr. Derrek R. Church – President (2000–2001) of the American Society of Neuroscientists.

Wendy S. Capegoat

She stood in line at the post office window in the Medical School, holding a bundle of letters to be mailed. As she looked around, she loudly uttered words only she understood, completely oblivious to those in front and back of her. At the time, no one, including Wendy, knew that a glioma was growing in her brain. As it grew inside her skull, it began pressing on certain regions of her brain, evoking involuntary, indecipherable speech.

It would be four years before she would succumb to this endogenous invader that took over her cerebral cortex and then her life. From undecipherable speech to a wheel chair to a complete loss of cognition, Wendy's deterioration progressed to a point where she had to spend the last several months of her life in a sanatorium. As the days went by, her bright blue eyes became dimmer and her body motionless. She died in her mid-forties on a cold, gloomy December day in 1999.

A devoted wife and a loyal employee, Wendy agreed to follow her boss, Dr. Frank I. M. Moral, as he assumed the chairmanship of the Neuroscience Department at the Jefferson University (JU) Medical School, Jefferson City, KS. She directed his laboratory at the State University of New Mexico (SUNM) for years and it was the right move for her. Dr. Moral needed someone reliable to look after his new research projects. She would oversee a larger staff and would have greater responsibilities as the director of the department chair's laboratory. Her husband, James, a computer technician, would have no problem moving to Kansas, too, as he would quickly find a new job. The couple moved to Kansas in the summer of 1987 when Wendy began her job as a Research Coordinator in the Neuroscience department at JU.

Lidia Quarry

Lidia Quarry, a brilliant and promising young assistant professor at Louisiana State University (LSU), was scanning the dozens of rows of poster exhibits at the Annual Meeting of the American Society of Neuroscientists that took place at the convention center in New Orleans, Louisiana, in November 1988.

After completing her postdoctoral training, performing research in one of the leading research laboratories on Alzheimer's disease in Ithaca, New York, Lidia had just accepted a faculty position at LSU. Others had tried to recruit her, including Dr. Frank I. M. Moral, who a year earlier assumed a departmental chairmanship at JU. However, she decided to follow her husband, a psychologist, who became a partner in an established clinic in Baton Rouge, LA, and thus, she joined the faculty at LSU.

Lidia received her elementary education in Pakistan and then was sent to England. She graduated from high school at age 16 and by the age when most people are still in college, she had already received her Ph.D. from Cambridge University.

As she was walking from one poster to the next, stopping to ask questions or to exchange ideas with their presenters, she felt a tap on her shoulder. Turning around she found herself facing Frank I.M. Moral, who had a big smile on his bearded face.

"Hello Lidia, how are you?" said Frank. "Oh, thank you, Dr. Moral, I am fine," said Lidia.

She thought to herself that Frank seemed to be awfully nice to her, considering that she had rejected the offer to join his department less than a year earlier. Soon she was to receive an explanation for this unexpected friendly gesture; Frank told her that his offer is still standing and that he is willing to make it even better for her to join him in Jefferson City.

Within eight months of that encounter with Dr. Moral, Lidia joined the faculty of the Neuroscience department at JU where she was given a large and well-equipped laboratory. As she already had two research grants by the time she left LSU, she had no difficulty attracting two excellent technicians to work under her, several graduate students and a postdoctoral fellow.

Lidia was well on her way to prominence as a researcher in the field of Alzheimer's disease.

Dr. Frank I. M. Moral

A graduate of Harvard University, Frank I. M. Moral has set his goals high. Although, a bit unusual for a scientist to do all his graduate work (master, doctoral and postdoctoral) in one institution, Frank completed it in five years and immediately landed his first academic position as an assistant professor at the State University of New Mexico (SUNM). About a decade later he was promoted to the rank of full professor at the Neuroscience Department there. Four years later, his big opportunity emerged with the resignation of the department's chair as Frank was appointed acting chairman.

Shortly thereafter, his colleagues in the department began to notice certain behavioral traits they had not noticed before. He became short-tempered, raising his voice in bursts of anger either in the presence of several faculty members or at one-on-one encounters. In several instances faculty members caught him contradicting previous statements he made, while in others he was caught lying. These behavioral oddities became more frequent as the time to select a new chairperson for the department approached.

Frank was one of the candidates for this position, an opportunity he had been looking and thriving for since he had joined the department. He had done everything he could to position himself as the top candidate for the job.

Despite administrative duties as an acting chairman, Frank had managed to assemble an impressive list of peer-reviewed publications, one of the key standards by which a scientist's stature is measured. A multi-year research grant from a French research foundation greatly enhanced Frank's chances to be chosen for his dream position, not to mention the two years he had served as acting chair. The search committee surely would take all these factors into consideration when the final decision is made. His anger outbursts would be understandable. After all, the pressure to publish and to receive funding for his research projects had been great and losing one's temper once in a while goes with the territory.

As it happened, the members of the search committee did not understand; they selected an "unknown" from Arizona. The committee members were greatly influenced by interviews they conducted with several faculty members in Frank's department. All those who were interviewed voiced their grave concerns about Dr. Moral's tendency to "bend the truth" and his vindictiveness against people who disagreed with him. They unanimously voiced their objection to Moral's candidacy.

Of course, following his defeat, Dr. Moral could not stand the idea of staying at SUNM as a regular faculty member or, for that matter, anywhere else. Once he tasted the taste of the power that comes with being a department chairman, nothing less would do. He had to find a chair position somewhere else. Frank hated the thought of moving away from New Mexico, nevertheless, he would not hesitate to move his home and family to another state given that a departmental chairmanship is at hand, even if it meant joining an obscure, lower-tier, university.

Searching the 'Positions Open' ad section in *Science*, one of the most prestigious scientific journals in the world, one particular ad caught his eye:

CHAIRPERSON
NEUROSCIENCE DEPARTMENT
MEDICAL SCHOOL
JEFFERSON UNIVERSITY
JEFFERSON CITY, KANSAS

The Jefferson University is searching for candidates to chair the Neuroscience Department at the Medical School. The successful applicant should have an earned doctorate or equivalent degree. Administrative experience and strong academic record demonstrating commitment to excellence in teaching and research is required. Must also demonstrate interpersonal and leadership skills. Screening will begin immediately and will continue until the position is filled.

Dr. Frank I.M. Moral applied for this position and eventually became the successful candidate. Seventeen years later, he is still the chairman of the Neuroscience Department at the medical school of JU.

Jeremy M. Artyr

Jeremy had dreamed of becoming a doctor. Being married to a physician had been a strong incentive to pursue such a career line. In 1992 he applied to the medical school at JU, but was not accepted.

As an alternative, Jeremy chose to do what many other students, when snubbed by the admission committee do, apply to the graduate school, obtain a Master degree in two years and then re-apply for medical school with a much better chance of being accepted.

The Neuroscience Department in the Medical School of JU has traditionally produced most of the graduates who later became medical students. Jeremy met with several faculty members in the department, including Dr. Lidia Quarry, Dr. Frank I. M. Moral and Dr. Keath H. Wright.

Jeremy was impressed with and excited about the scientific project that Dr. Quarry suggested. She had been working at the time on an animal model of Alzheimer's disease and was looking for ways to develop a stem cell line, which originates from the diseased animal itself, to be implanted in the affected brain regions. The idea was that such stem cells would begin to divide and take over for the dying Alzheimer cells. Additional expertise was required in both physiology and microscopy to carry out this ambitious project since such stem cells had to be identified both morphologically and functionally before and after their conversion.

Dr. Quarry reiterated to Jeremy that such a project could not be completed in 18 to 24 months, and that he should consider applying for a Doctoral rather than a Masters degree in the department, Additionally, he should be ready to invest 36 to 48 months to complete his doctorate.

Jeremy wanted to have some time to consider his options. His enthusiasm about the project and the encouragement of his family made his decision easier; medical school could wait for four years while he delved into one of the most intriguing and mysterious brain disorders to inflict the human race.

Soon after their first meeting, Jeremy told Dr. Quarry that he had decided to pursue his Ph.D. degree, working on his thesis in her laboratory under her mentorship. Together they went to meet Dr. Keath H. Wright, a full professor and a real genius who had been the most underrated scientist in the medical school. He agreed to mentor Jeremy on the physiology part of the project.

Jeremy and Dr. Quarry later met with Dr. Frank I.M. Moral who tightly controls the microscopy facilities of the department.

At the end of the day, everything was set for Jeremy to begin his exciting journey into the secrets of the debilitating affliction known as Alzheimer's disease.

The only thing left to do to complete the process of his becoming a graduate student in the Neuroscience Department was to select two additional members for his thesis committee. Dr. Quarry suggested a colleague of hers in the Anesthesiology Department, while Dr. Moral suggested Dr. Christian C. Heat from the Neurology Department. Both gladly agreed to serve on Jeremy's thesis committee.

The Whistleblower (Dr. W)

As Dr. W. was sitting in his small, cramped office, engrossed in statistical calculations of his latest experiments, the telephone on his desk rang. He picked up the receiver and said: "Good morning." He heard Lidia's voice with her slight foreign accent: "May I come to see you? I must show you something."

Dr. W. and Lidia had known each other for a decade and had mutual research interests. Back in 1988, Frank I. M. Moral asked him to interview Lidia for an opening in the Neuroscience Department. As an Associate in Moral's department, Dr. W. interviewed many of the new candidates, as Frank trusted and relied on his judgment, including his strong recommendation that Lidia be hired for the open position.

As Lidia assumed that position after her short stint at LSU, Dr. W. was proud to see her flourishing and succeeding beyond all expectations. She had asked him, and he always agreed, to serve on thesis committees of her graduate students.

Several minutes after her telephone call, she stood at his open office door, her dark eyes moist and her voice trembling.

"May I close the door behind me?" she asked. "Sure, come in" he said, pointing to an empty chair.

Sitting down she handed him a folder containing a 30-page-thick paper file and said: "Look! Moral submitted a grant proposal based on my work and it got funded. He never told me about it or asked me to join him. He stole my research and used my ideas."

By now she was sobbing.

Two names appeared at the top of the first page of the grant proposal Lidia handed him, Frank I. M. Moral, Ph.D., and Christian C. Heat, M.D. The latter, a neurologist and Vice Chairman of the Neurology Department, had had established scientific and administrative collaborations with Dr. Moral for several years.

Trying to calm her down as he scanned through the pages of a small print, single-spaced text, Dr. W. asked softly:

"What do you mean by saying that Moral stole your research?" Her reply was almost a shout: "He did! Look at the work that is cited, the preliminary experiments, the ideas for future experiments, all of these are mine."

There was desperation in her voice and a painful look on her face. Dr. W. knew that somehow he must help her find the strength to fight the dreadful feeling of complete despair.

Lidia believed that she was robbed of her career and her intellectual property. She was convinced that the person who recruited her, the one who for several years was her greatest supporter and cheerleader, had done it.

"I need some time to look at the proposal. I need some time to think and consider your options, Lidia. I will call you tomorrow". Dr. W. said to her.

She stood up with her shoulders slumped and slowly stepped out of his office, leaving the folder with him.

Dr. W. had never encountered, until that moment, a wrong doing in science of such proportion.

Having a father who was a police criminologist and a mother who was a teacher for many decades, he grew up watching and experiencing the pursuit of justice and the punishment of the wrongdoer. Police stories, common around the dinner table, always ended with the moral that the crime does not pay. His affinity to science undoubtedly came from his father. For him, science had been the realization of the purest way to pursue the truth.

Dr. W. sat quietly for several minutes, trying to digest the potentially scandalous revelation that was lying in front of him. Would Frank Moral really do something so blatant? At his position, what had he to gain? If Lidia's accusations were true, Frank Moral would have so much more to lose than to gain. The whole situation seemed unimaginable.

Dr. W. began reading the proposal. It was submitted in September 1996 to a local foundation of one of the hospitals in Jefferson City. The requested amount was almost $100,000 and was approved for funding by the foundation eight months after its submission. A letter from the foundation was attached, addressed to Christian C. Heat and Frank I. M. Moral, informing them that the trustees of the foundation approved this grant award to them. Following several pages of biographical sketches of the two principal investigators and that of a graduate student who would perform the majority of the lab work, the body of the proposal itself began with an introduction.

He read through the **Introduction** section followed by the **Specific Aims** of the study and then, as he was reading the **Background and Significance** section, a strange sensation of familiarity fell over him. It was as if he had already read this very text before. Page after page, there was text that he knew had been written neither by Frank I. M. Moral nor by Christian C. Heat.

Dr. W. removed Jeremy M. Artyr's doctoral thesis from a shelf in his office, opened it at the **Background** section and begun comparing its text with the text of Moral and Heat's grant proposal. Word by word, line after line, paragraph after paragraph, page after page, the grant proposal's text was identical to the text of Artyr's thesis. Nowhere to be found in the grant proposal was a reference to Artyr's thesis.

W. was sitting motionless in his chair for a very long time. The unexpected, shocking revelation that the chairmen of two major departments in his medical school had engaged in plagiarizing from a doctoral thesis of their own student kept him numb, unable to think straight and unsure what, if any, one should do about it.

Guidelines and Definitions

Like all academic institutions receiving federal funds, JU is required to have many rules according to which its academic and scientific affairs are managed and controlled. These rules are compiled into one book, the *Blue Book.* Another document that has been used at the medical school and was borrowed from a similar document at Harvard University is entitled "Guidelines and Reference Material for the Ethical Conduct and Reporting of Scientific Research and Procedures for Dealing with Allegations of Scientific Misconduct." The preface of this document reads:

> *"Academic institutions are unique among institutions in that their principal "products" are the search of the truth and its dissemination. It thus follows that all university activities be characterized by honesty and integrity and that compromising these traits cannot be tolerated. The trust and support of the community depend on the continued demonstration by the institution that its activities are truthful and honest, that its "products" are reliable, and that it has in place an effective and fair mechanism for promoting ethical behavior and for dealing with allegations of unethical conduct. All members of the academic community are expected to maintain the highest possible ethical standards for the conduct and reporting of research and to communicate them, both directly and by example, to all those who come under their influence."*

The "Guidelines" were developed by several leading universities and adopted by the Medical School of JU. Misconduct in science is defined by the "Guidelines" in three terms as follows:

1. *Plagiarism – using others' data (or ideas) without acknowledging the source;*
2. *Fabrication – inventing or counterfeiting data;*
3. *Falsification – altering data.*

The National Academy of Sciences (NAS) also published a booklet entitled "On Being a Scientist; Responsible Conduct in Research"[1] in which the definition of two out of the three misconduct terms is similar, however, the definition of "plagiarism" is somewhat different:

"Plagiarism – using the ideas or words of another person without giving appropriate credit."

Thus, JU guidelines do not define *"using the words of others"* as plagiarism. Nevertheless, these guidelines also apply to the preparation of grant applications and it specifically states that honesty and integrity in applying for research funds represent the only acceptable approach.

The second part of the guidelines lists the procedures for dealing with allegations of unethical conduct that should be examined in four successive stages, each of which will be carried out expeditiously and in credible manner, with emphasis on due process, protection of individual rights and maintenance of confidentiality. The first (Preliminary) and the second stage (Initial) comprise the Phase of Inquiry and the third (Formal) and fourth stage (Resolution) constitutes the Phase of Investigation.

In the Preliminary Stage, allegations of misconduct may be made to the Ombudsman of the medical school either orally or in writing.

Notes

[1] On Being a Scientist – Responsible Conduct in Research. Committee on Science, Engineering and Public Policy, National Academy of Sciences, National Academy of Engineering, Institute of Medicine. National Academy Press, Washington, D.C. 1995

The Ombudsman

A quiet and well-mannered physician in his early seventies, he still devotes much of his time to his patients and, in addition, finds time for his colleagues and his profession. In the years since he was appointed Ombudsman of the Medical School at JU, Dr. George O. M. Budsman never handled an official complaint of scientific misconduct.

Budsman was sitting in his office, facing the whistleblower at the other side of his paper-cluttered desk. His lack of experience in this matter was apparent as he frequently referred to "The Guidelines."

In front of him lay an unsigned letter dated July 1, 1998. He and the whistleblower spoke on the telephone a day earlier and agreed to meet in the ombudsman's office the next day. The letter was addressed to Budsman and reported a case of misconduct in science that involved plagiarism and falsification. It described the grant proposal submitted by Drs. Moral and Heat to a local foundation dated October 15, 1996 and the fact that it was approved and funded on July 14, 1997.

It went on to state that the experiments proposed in this proposal are based on a doctoral research thesis performed, written and defended by Dr. Jeremy M. Artyr under the mentorship of Drs. Quarry, Wright and Moral, and that part of the results included in the thesis were published. At the second half of the one-page letter, the whistleblower wrote:

"To my astonishment, I discovered that many passages, paragraphs, and statements that are included in the above-mentioned grant proposal were copied verbatim from Dr. Artyr's thesis. No credit was given anywhere in the grant proposal to Dr. Artyr and in no place in the grant proposal his thesis has been cited. I also found one example of falsification where Dr. Moral, in his biographical sketch, claims to be a member, from 1988 to the present, of a National Institute of Health (NIH) BSBS Study Section. The NIH informed me that they do not have a BSBS Study Section. After giving these issues of scientific misconduct a long and very painful consideration, I have decided to officially file this report."

After agreeing that everything included in the report is according to the guidelines, Budsman told the whistleblower that he would deliver the report that afternoon to the dean of the Medical School, Dr. Dean A. Verage.

Dr. Dean A. Verage

Dean A. Verage had been the dean of the Medical School at JU since 1982. His selection for this position was a process of compromise. A pathologist with very little research productivity and even less administrative experience, Dr. Verage was elected Dean of the Medical School to replace his resigning predecessor.

Verage's job performance evaluation in 1997, a process each faculty member must go through every 5 years, had received an unsatisfactory grade based on a questionnaire that was distributed among all faculty members of the medical school. Despite that, Verage's review committee, headed by Dr. Harvey L. Powerhouse, Chairman, Neurology Department, recommended a five-year extension of Verage's contract, a recommendation that was accepted by the university Board of Trustees.

The ombudsman had just delivered to Dean A. Verage an anonymous report. The dean, too, had never dealt with a case of misconduct in science. He thus read the "Guidelines" and learned that he should conduct an informal inquiry to determine whether the complaint warranted further attention or should be dropped. He also learned that this inquiry should include a consultation with the accused and that a report of this inquiry should be sent within 14 calendar days to the ombudsman who would deliver it immediately to the complainant (the whistleblower) and the accused.

Verage immediately decided to delegate most of the burden of the process to two of his associates, Vice Dean for Academic Affairs, Donald V. Icedean, Ph.D., and Associate Dean for Research, Bertha I. Clash, Ph.D, who also had been an associate in the Neuroscience Department which was chaired by one of the accused, Frank I. M. Moral. Thus, right from the start, the process of handling this case of scientific misconduct was flawed as Clash clearly had a conflict of interest. At best, Verage's choice could be an oversight on his part, at worse, the beginning of a cover-up.

Icedean and Clash did not consult with the accused until August 13, 1998, 42 days after the official filing of the complaint, a violation of the 14-calendar-days requirement for completion of the Preliminary Stage and a bad sign for things to come.

On the same day, Moral and Heat responded to the misconduct allegations in a letter to Dr. Icedean, Vice Dean for Academic Affairs. In their letter they said:

> "...we are surprised and disappointed that a distorted one-sided version has been given. We wonder for what hidden purpose or gain could this complaint have been made? For the record, the grant proposal we submitted clearly was an academic endeavor and we consider it our responsibility to continue work that Dr. Moral conceived of many years ago which was carried under his primary direction and almost exclusively in his lab."

This opening statement of their letter contains two misrepresentations. First, the work the grant proposal proposed to pursue was not the brainchild of Dr. Moral. It was the idea of Dr. Quarry.

A quick glance into Moral's list of publications would reveal not even one paper dealing with either Alzheimer's disease or with transplantation, the two topics with which Dr. Artyr's thesis dealt.

Additionally, Dr. Moral was not Dr. Artyr's primary mentor. Dr. Quarry was his mentor and the reason for the work being performed mainly in her lab was the fact that the project was funded by research grants awarded to Dr. Quarry. Actually, on the only paper published based on Artyr's work, he is listed as the first author, Quarry listed second, Wright is third and Moral is listed last. The paper also acknowledges "the work was supported by a Federal Grant awarded to Dr. Quarry."

Moreover, immediately after his thesis defense presentation, Dr. Artyr stepped out of the auditorium where the presentation had taken place, and left the five members of his dissertation committee, Drs. Quarry, Wright, Moral, Heat and W, to reach a decision on awarding him his doctoral degree. While the five were unanimously impressed with both the research and its presentation, Dr. Moral was the one who voiced what every one on the committee felt very strongly about, namely, that this research project must continue.

Frank I. M. Moral turned to Dr. Quarry and said: "Lidia, this is a beautiful work and you must submit as soon as possible an NIH grant application based on Jeremy's findings."

That was in April 1996. Less than five months later Drs. Moral and Heat secretly used Artyr's thesis to submit a grant proposal of their own, leaving out Drs. Quarry and Wright.

The letter by Moral and Heat to Dr. Icedean continued:

"There is no doubt that a substantial portion of the background and significance sections of our proposal as well as parts of the preliminary results come directly from Jeremy M. Artyr's thesis. A peer-reviewed manuscript and four of Dr. Artyr's published abstracts were referenced. The thesis was not referenced because the key issues had been published and because thesis availability is at best extremely limited."

Thus, the most important issue in the whistleblower's complaint, namely, plagiarism, was openly admitted in the letter of Moral and Heat. After the admission was made, they simply tried to justify their misconduct with unacceptable excuses, claiming that they referenced Artyr's lone paper and his abstracts and not the thesis due to the latter's limited availability. Is limited availability a justification for not crediting an author's work?

In their letter, Moral and Heat also relate to the falsification mentioned in the complaint. They wrote:

"The claim of falsification in Dr. Moral's biographical sketch is misleading. Dr. Moral served on the NIH BSBS Study Section for many years. When he resigned his tenure on that Study Section, his CV (Curriculum Vita) was apparently not updated, and the CV submitted (with the grant proposal) merely reflects an oversight concerning the date."

Interestingly, Dr. I. M. Moral submitted another grant proposal later in 1998, two years after the questioned proposal was submitted and a few months after the misconduct complaint was filed, and in it his biographical sketch still contained the misleading information regarding his NIH duties.

Moral and Heat ended their letter as follows:

"We trust that this description demonstrates our academic honesty, our genuine commitment to our research, and the

dismay we feel when that honesty and commitment are called into question."

On August 18, 1998, 47 days after the original complaint was filed and not 14 days as required by the "Guidelines", Verage received a letter from Icedean and Clash, who also attached the letter of Moral and Heat. In their letter to Dr. Dean A. Verage, Drs. Icedean and Clash repeated almost verbatim all the points that Moral and Heat raised and in conclusion said:

"...After having thoroughly reviewed these allegations, we conclude the complaint warrants no further investigation and that the inquiry should not proceed to the next stage."

On August 24, 1998, a copy of that letter was also sent to the Ombudsman who copied it to the whistleblower.

Clearly, the administrators of the Medical School at JU did not follow closely the "Guidelines on Handling Allegations of Unethical Research Activities," an incident that had repeated numerous times during the investigation and the processing of this case. Nevertheless, the whistleblower was expected to follow these very "Guidelines" to the dot.

Simon Wall

The "Guidelines" specify that:

> "...if the Inquiry's report is not satisfactory to the complainant, he or she will so inform the Ombudsman within 3 calendar days of receiving the report. The Ombudsman shall notify the Dean and the Inquiry shall proceed to the Initial Stage within 8 calendar days."

The "Guidelines" also specify the following:

> "The individual making the formal allegation must provide a brief, signed statement of the charge to the Dean with a copy to the Ombudsman."

Upon receiving a copy of the Inquiry's Preliminary Stage report, the whistleblower had to make a decision whether or not to pursue it further.

The report was completely unsatisfactory. Frank I. M. Moral and Christian C. Heat were getting away with "murder." At the time the whistleblower filed his anonymous complaint, Lidia Quarry had already told him that things were changing fast in the Neuroscience Department. Dr. Moral's attitude toward her had become cold and unfriendly. He had just transferred her to teach a different course to medical students with which she was completely unfamiliar, and frequently criticized her teaching, something he had never done in the past.

Lidia won a teaching award just two years earlier and a plaque commemorating that award was hanging proudly on the wall in her office. She confided to the whistleblower that she believed the submission of the grant proposal behind her back was but the first step in Moral's plan to end her scientific career at JU. Frank Moral became short-tempered with her, raising his voice more frequently than ever, at times in front of other colleagues, or even in front of her own lab people.

Regardless of Lidia's problems, the decision as to whether to pursue the complaint further or to drop the whole affair had to be made based solely on the merit of the case of misconduct itself.

27

It was absolutely clear to the whistleblower that plagiarism had been committed. Moral and Heat actually admitted as much in their letter to Dr. Donald V. Icedean, Associate Dean for Academic affairs.

Long before he submitted his anonymous complaint, the whistleblower spoke with no less than five of his colleagues, both in his own and in other departments. Without revealing any of the specifics of the misconduct case to them, each one, after hearing the general details, had warned him of possible negative ramifications that could impact his own career at the university. The general consensus after talking with his colleagues was that the administration will do everything in its power to quell any bad publicity for the university by sweeping the case under the carpet and, if necessary, by silencing the whistleblower himself.

Nevertheless, he was the one who happened to discover that a flagrant scientific misconduct was committed by a chairman and a vice chairman of two principal departments. He could not knowingly ignore such a blatant transgression and pretend as if scientific research at JU is *"seeking the truth and its dissemination."*

On August 27, 1998, a one-page official complaint against Drs. Frank I. M. Moral and Christian C. Heat alleging scientific misconduct was delivered to Dr. George O. M. Budsman. A signature appeared at the bottom of the complaint above the name Simon Wall, Ph.D., Professor of Anesthesiology. Dr. Budsman delivered it, yet again, to Dr. Dean A. Verage, the dean of the Medical School at JU.

Simon Wall sat in his office, lamenting over the events of the past weeks. In his 30 years as a scientist, this was the first case of serious scientific misconduct he had personally encountered.

Somewhat naively, he had never considered the possibility that scientists would engage in an act that could taint their own scientific work, let alone their name, and possibly the work of others. Even more shocking for him was the fact that the two who committed this breach of trust were among the leaders of the institution.

Although, at the time of the grant proposal submission Dr. Heat was the vice chairman of his department, by July 1998, he had already assumed its chairmanship. He won the position over many excellent candidates who applied for that position and were interviewed at length for the job a year earlier. It was, however, but a foregone conclusion for those who followed the staged selection process, that Heat would, eventually, become the next chairman of the Neurology Department.

As has been mentioned earlier, Harvey L. Powerhouse, the previous chairman, who served on the job for over 20 years, was ready to retire. He had built and had expanded the department with Dr. Heat, his 15 years junior, from a small division of the Surgery Department into a separate, independent entity. Powerhouse wanted to assure that Heat inherited his job.

However, a departmental chairperson, as in any other high profile job in academia, is selected only after an exhaustive search process done by a committee that interviews several candidates and recommends one of them to the dean. Once the dean accepts the recommendation of the committee, the selected candidate has to be approved by the faculty members of his future department. As has been pointed out already, the Dean, Dr. Verage, went through a review process of his own job performance only two years earlier and received an unsatisfactory grade. It was Dr. Powerhouse who chaired Verage's Review Committee and he was the one who recommended that the contract of the dean be renewed for an additional five years.

Dr. Dean A. Verage got his wish and stayed as the Dean of the Medical School until the end of 1999. However, this contract renewal had a price tag, a deal between Powerhouse and Verage in which the former was assured by the latter that Dr. Heat would be the next chairman of the Neurology Department.

In 1997, upon the announcement of Dr. Powerhouse's retirement, Dr. Verage nominated Dr. Frank I. M. Moral as the Chairman of the Search Committee for a new head of the Neurology Department. Dr. Christian C. Heat, of course, was one of the candidates. Moral's selection as chair of the search committee was another flagrant conflict of interest as he and Heat were and continue to be, as evident from their grant proposal, close collaborators. They were also close friends. Although, the dean was aware of these relationships, it did not prevent him from selecting Moral for that duty.

Moral's agreed to chair the search committee, despite it being a flagrant conflict of interest, for two important reasons: first, Powerhouse, and later Heat, had great influence on how large a slice of the pie of funds assigned to "The KS Head and Spine Injury Panel" was to be divided among Kansas' researchers who submit applications for research grants to the panel.

The Kansas legislature had passed a law allowing a certain percentage of each paid traffic violation to be earmarked for funds allocated to the panel and hence to the authors of the successful grant proposals submitted to the panel.

Most grants are awarded for an average of three years at approximately $100,000 per year per grant. Drs. Moral and Heat had submitted a grant proposal every three years beginning in 1995 and were successful in getting a grant approved every time they applied. Many faculty members and residents in Heat's department have also been the "lucky" awardees. Other researchers in other departments were not as successful, including Simon Wall.

Thus, Dr. Moral had very good reasons to accept his nomination by the dean to chair the search committee for a new chairperson for the Neurology Department. By agreeing to do so, Moral was in control of the selection process. Moreover, he was instructed by Verage to recommend two finalists to him, one of whom should be Heat. Moral was more than glad to oblige. And thus, Heat was selected as the new Chairman of the Neurology Department.

Hence, Simon Wall stood alone against two departmental chairmen. However, even more daunting was the fact that at JU, since 1989, a departmental chairperson has been both a faculty member and an administrator, an unusual hybrid that rules over his/her faculty members without the latter having any real power in deciding the future of their leader even when his/her performance is unsatisfactory. This is in contrast to most academic institutions where faculty members have the absolute power to determine who leads them.

Concomitantly, at JU, chairpersons were placed at the bottom of the administration's pyramid, giving deans, the provost, vice presidents and the president, total control over chairpersons and, through them, over faculty members.

Slowly, the grim reality of being alone, isolated, and completely unprepared for the battles that were surely to come, overtook Simon. He knew that once his name became known to the accused, all hell would break lose.

In the weeks and months that followed, Simon found himself thinking about his late father. Leo Wall was an honest man who strictly disciplined his three sons to follow his example. Many a time he emphasized to them the importance of one's reputation, much more important than material riches. Simon tried to imagine his father's actions in a similar situation only to realize that no matter what his father would do, the deal was complete and things were now set in motion.

According to the "Guidelines and Reference Material for the Ethical Conduct and Reporting of Research and Procedures for Dealing with Allegations of Scientific Misconduct"

The dean has 8 calendar days to appoint a fact-finding Review Panel the purpose of which is to determine whether an investigation of the complaint is warranted. The Panel shall consist of three tenured faculty members with experience relevant to the complaint being investigated. These individuals cannot be from any department in which the Accused holds appointment or having responsibility for any portion of the activity being questioned. The Panel shall select its own Chair, who will be responsible for seeing that minutes are kept and for formulating the Panel's report.

Within 35 calendar days of the establishment of the Review Panel, its Chair will forward the report of the Panel to the Dean, with copies to the Ombudsman, the Accused and the Complainant. The report shall contain the Panel's recommendation that the charges be dropped or that an investigation be held. In either instance, reasons for the recommendation must be stated in writing. Issuance of the report shall complete the Initial Stage.

The Dean will determine whether the report of the Review Panel warrants progression to the Formal Stage and shall, within 30 calendar days, issue a written determination to the Ombudsman, the Accused and the Complainant, and appoint an Investigative Board, if necessary.

Until now, only Drs. Quarry and Wall have seen the extent of the scientific misconduct committed by Moral and Heat. Neither the dean nor his two associates had asked to look at the evidence. Thus, the members of the Review Panel would have been the only other faculty members, besides Quarry and Wall, to see the evidence. Much of Simon Wall's confidence in the wisdom of his decision to blow the whistle was hanging on the Review Panel's judgment.

The Review Panel

On September 8, 1998, Dr. Dean A. Verage appointed a three-member Review Panel to conduct the initial stage of the investigation into the allegation of a scientific misconduct by Drs. Frank I. M. Moral and Christian C. Heat. Verage closed his appointment letter to each of the Panel members with the following line:

This is an extremely important task, and I appreciate your willingness to serve.

On September 12, 1998, Dr. Simon Wall delivered a package accompanied by a letter to the Panel that contained all the information and evidence he had gathered on the case, including several of his arguments regarding the response letter of Drs. Moral and Heat in the preliminary stage.

Simon Wall also sent a copy of that letter to Dr. David O.K. Yesmam, Associate Provost of JU. Wall chose Dr. Yesmam as an additional academic figure to whom he disseminates the information, since he was somewhat dubious about the will of the Medical School administration to take on the case and to conduct a full investigation.

On October 2, 1998, the Review Panel sent its report to Dr. Verage with copies to Drs. Budsman, the Ombudsman at JU, Frank I. M. Moral, Professor and Chair, Neuroscience Department, Christian C. Heat, Professor and Chair, Neurology Department, and Simon Wall, Professor, Anesthesiology Department.

The three-page report reviewed the history of the case and the two specific allegations and then continued as follows:

According to the 'Guidelines', the Panel has only two options to recommend to the Dean: (1) that the charges be dropped or (2) that a formal investigation of the allegation(s) be held.

Allegation (1)

Because of the appearance of plagiarism, as defined by 'Graduate Bulletin of the Jefferson University," the panel recommends that a formal investigation of allegation 1, plagiarism of Dr. J. M. Artyr's thesis, be held. The evidence

34

supplied indicates to us that Drs. Moral and Heat incorporated significant portions of Dr. Artyr's thesis into the grant application without acknowledging the author. Drs. Moral and Heat in their letter of August 13, 1998 to Dr. Icedean acknowledged copying sections of Dr. Artyr's thesis into the grant application. The Panel believes that references in the grant application to the published paper and abstracts, or references to 'our studies,' are not adequate substitutes for acknowledgement of quoting Dr. Artyr's words as written in his thesis.

In making this recommendation, the Panel explored in considerable details the definition and implications of the term 'plagiarism.' The 'Guidelines' define plagiarism as 'using others' data (or ideas) without acknowledging the source.'

The 'Graduate Bulletin of the Jefferson University' defines plagiarism as (among others things): 'Exactly reproducing someone else's words without identifying the words with quotation marks or by appropriate indentation, or without properly citing the quotation in a footnote or reference.'

The National Academy of Sciences report entitled 'On becoming a Scientist,' which is required reading for many new graduate students, states in a section on plagiarism that 'The intentional use of another's intellectual property without giving credit may seem more blameworthy than the actions of a person who claims to have plagiarized because of inattention or sloppiness. But as in the case of fraud, the harm to the victim is the same regardless of intention. Furthermore, given the difficulty of judging intentions, the censure imposed by the scientific community is likely to be equally great.[2]

The Panel discussed at length potential ambiguities concerning ownership of intellectual property in collaborative projects. Most scientists would agree on joint ownership of ideas and data in collaborative efforts. However, the relationship between a student and a mentor may be especially prone to misunderstandings or misinterpretations regarding intellectual ownership. It is unclear to the Panel whether a thesis is the sole intellectual property of the student. The 'Guidelines' unfortunately provide no insight into this question. In the experience of the Panel members, the mentor usually has considerable input into the writing of a thesis. This input may take many forms–from verbal advice to extensive editing and/or rewriting the student's words. The editing process might make the mentor feel entitled to use passages from the thesis without attribution. However, in the opinion of the panel members, a student is potentially the more vulnerable member of the student-mentor relationship and should be protected from misappropriation of his or her intellectual property.

After due deliberation, the Panel believes that an investigation of the allegation of plagiarism is warranted. The Panel strongly feels that all faculty members (especially department chairs as intellectual leaders of their departments) should operate with the highest standards of integrity.

<u>*Allegation (2)*</u>

The Panel recommends that the charge that Dr. Moral falsified membership on an NIH study section be dropped. We find Dr. Moral's statement of oversight in his letter of August 13, 1998 to Dr. Icedean to be reasonable and convincing.

October 1, 1998

Signed: Members of the Review Panel

Upon first reading this report, Simon felt great relief. Here were three other academic professors who, upon reviewing the evidence, concluded that plagiarism did indeed take place. He read the report twice more before an alarm went off in his head. For the first time Simon had noticed a significant difference in the definition of 'plagiarism' by the "Guidelines" used by the Medical School of JU and those used by the "Graduate Bulletin of JU." While the latter defines *plagiarism* as *"Exactly reproducing someone else's **words** without identifying the words with quotation marks or by appropriate indentation, or without* *properly citing the quotation in a footnote or reference,"* the former defines it as *"using others' **data** (or ideas) without acknowledging the source."*

If someone chooses to be picky regarding definitions, **words** and **data** are not synonymous. Simon tried to put these thoughts aside, but **words** and **data** kept ringing in his ears. It had never occurred to him before to check the data that Moral and Heat used in their grant proposal. He compared only the text of the grant proposal with that of Artyr's thesis, not the many data points in the two documents.

He opened a drawer of one of his file cabinets and removed a folder containing a copy of the grant proposal. From a bookshelf above him he brought down his own copy of Artyr's thesis and began browsing the two documents.

In the **Preliminary Results** section of the grant proposal, a table listed counts of cells in cultures after treating mice *in situ* to cause regeneration of cells in a specific nucleus in the central nervous system. Moral and Heat claimed that in Artyr's study, which they relate to as

...in our previous study, these counts were extremely variable between animals within the same treatment groups, which made the approach unreliable and thus required large sample size.

To justify this claim and the need for funds to improve the method such that variability would be minimized, they had reconstructed the table using Artyr's data in his thesis. The table that appeared in the grant proposal was published neither in the one paper by Artyr et al., nor in any of his abstracts. The table in the grant proposal was constructed by consolidating two consecutive tables from Artyr's thesis. Moral and Heat had combined counts of two different types of cells, each listed separately in the two tables in the thesis, into one inclusive table in the grant proposal boosting their claim of high variability.

They, of course, did not reference the thesis regarding these data, and by combining the counts of two different types of cells into one table that does not distinguish between them, they have actually committed a fabrication.

Thus, Simon Wall discovered that Frank I. M. Moral and Christian C. Heat committed plagiarism even according to the "Guidelines" of JU Medical School, that define it as: *Using others' data (or ideas) without acknowledging the source.*

Hence, to his surprise, Simon uncovered an additional commission of scientific misconduct by Moral and Heat, namely, *fabrication: inventing or counterfeiting data.*

Simon wondered: "if these two plagiarists have already decided to commit their deed, why would they copy exactly the original numbers from Artyr's thesis to create a new table? Why not try to hide it better?" For instance, Moral and Heat copied pairs of numbers, 945 and 1166, from Artyr's two tables and in the table of the grant application they placed the number 2111, the exact sum of the two. If they had simply used the number 2108 or 2113 instead of 2111, their plagiarism of data could never have been detected.

Still, there was one very important question that remained unanswered. Why would Moral and Heat risk so much by plagiarizing Artyr's thesis when they could easily use the published paper of Artyr's work, a paper of which Moral is a coauthor, and risk nothing?

Their motive, then an enigma to Wall, once understood, would provide a valuable insight into the mindset of the unethical scientist and his/her set of priorities. Most importantly, it would enable academicians of all ranks to develop a curriculum that includes the teaching of ethical and honest conduct of scientific research.

The scientific publication by Jeremy M. Artyr and his colleagues is a more concise and better-written document than his thesis. Why not use it in preparing the grant proposal, even verbatim, which would not be considered plagiarism? Why the two, Moral and Heat, chose instead to plagiarize a document of a lesser quality? What other differences existed between the scientific publication and the thesis, which made them use the latter rather than the former? Dr. Wall scanned the reprint of the publication by Artyr et al., as he was contemplating these questions.

The study was published in *Journal of Brain Research.* Under the title were listed the authors, J. M. Artyr, L. Quarry, K.H. Wright, F. I. M. Moral, followed by the **Abstract,** then **Introduction, Materials and Methods, Results, Discussion, Acknowledgements** and **References.** He read the paper for the third time, but could not uncover any hint for Moral and Heat's reasoning for using the thesis rather than the paper in their proposal preparation.

Then, just as he was about to give up, it hit him: "the **Acknowledgements!** This is it!" The acknowledgements listed very clearly everything that one needed to know about who was the principal player in Artyr's thesis. It specifically listed the support of LQ (Lidia Quarry) by a USPHS grant (with a specific NS number). She was the one who provided most of the funding for the project, her project; the ideas, her ideas; the laboratory space, her laboratory. If Moral and Heat had used the paper as their main source they could face a real challenge from Dr. Quarry, since the main researcher behind the project had been clearly indicated. Instead, by using Artyr's thesis they avoided such a challenge. More importantly, in using their own explanation (in their letter to Dean Verage) for not referencing the thesis in their grant proposal (*"The thesis was not referenced because the key issues had been published and because the thesis availability is at best extremely limited"*) they were counting on the *"extremely limited availability"* of the thesis to avoid the exposure of their misconduct.

Suddenly, everything made sense, a sinister one. What is the best way to plagiarize safely if not from a source extremely limited in availability? What is the sure way to avoid any challenge if not by plagiarizing the work of your own student who is no longer working with you and who, once told about the incident, actually felt flattered by the fact that two chairmen had copied his own words into their grant proposal?

Moreover, once the grant proposal was funded, the change in Moral's attitude toward Lidia Quarry also made sense. Since he now had funds that would enable him to take over her project, there was no place for both of them in the same department. Actually, there was no way he and Heat could carry out this research while Dr. Quarry was still part of the Neuroscience Department, since sooner or later she would discover these facts and would blow the whistle. Thus, the great efforts by Dr. Frank I. M Moral to make life in his department unbearable for Dr. Quarry were the only way to push her out. Furthermore, Simon Wall understood Lidia's outrage much better now.

With somewhat clearer picture as to actions and reactions in this complicated case of scientific misconduct, Simon Wall could do nothing, but to wait for Dr. Dean A. Verage's decision on the recommendation of the Review Panel.

Notes

[2] *Proc. Natl. Acad. Sci. USA,* **86**, 9071, 1989a

Crime and Punishment

On October 24, 1998, Dr. Barry A. L. Truist, Professor and Chair, Anesthesiology Department, received the following letter:

Dear Barry,

I am writing to inform you that the Dean's office is temporarily reallocating the research lab located in room 811 of the Research Building to the Neurology Department effective November 3, 1998.

This space will again become vacant when the new Research Building is completed in September 2000. At that time, the Anesthesiology Department will be given the opportunity to request the return of this allocation of space back to your department. Our Physical Plant Director will get in touch with Dr. Simon Wall to make arrangement for the relocation of items currently being stored in the lab.

Your cooperation is greatly appreciated.

Sincerely,

Dean A. Verage, M.D.
Dean, Medical School
Jefferson University

Dr. Truist immediately sent a copy of Verage's letter to Simon Wall. Research space has always been hard to come by at JU, as is the case in many other institutions. All space in the Medical School is controlled by the Dean's office and is assigned as needed to different departments. The Dean retains control over assigned space and can reassign it at any time without as much as a letter to the department's chair.

When Simon read the letter he could not help but remember the warnings he had heard from those with whom he consulted prior to filing his complaint. The research space he was about to lose had been used by one of his graduate students who had worked on her doctoral degree from 1997 to 2000.

He explained to Barry Truist his dilemma, namely the fact that he had no other space for the student to perform her experiments. Dr. Truist conveyed this concern to Verage, but to no avail. Hence, it was clear that a line had been drawn in the sand.

Dean Verage perceived Simon Wall as the culprit in this case, the one who was out to blemish the institute's reputation, a trouble maker whose deeds should be punishable not only by taking research space away from him, regardless of his productivity and his students' needs, but to add insult to injury, transfer his space to the department whose chair has been accused of scientific misconduct.

Would this punishment mean that a decision had already been made regarding the allegation of misconduct in science? Was this just the first in a string of retributions against Simon Wall, the whistleblower? He could easily guess what Verage's determination would be on the report of the Review Panel even before receiving a notification about it.

On November 4, 1998, a day after Simon Wall vacated one of his labs as ordered, Dr. Dean A. Verage sent the following letter to Dr. George Budsman, Ombudsman:

George O. M. Budsman M.D.
Ombudsman
Medical School

RE: Allegations of Unethical Research Activities in the Medical School

Dear Dr. Budsman:

This represents my written determination concerning the report of the Review Panel charged with conducting an inquiry into allegations by Dr. Simon Wall of scientific misconduct by Drs. Frank I. M. Moral and Christian C. Heat. In a report dated October 2, 1998, received in my office on October 7, 1998, the Panel recommended that the charge that Dr. Moral falsified membership on an NIH Study Section be dropped. I accept the Panel's recommendation on this allegation, which is dismissed.

41

On the remaining allegation of plagiarism the Panel recommends that a formal investigation be conducted. In arriving at a determination on the allegations, I thoroughly reviewed the original complaint of Dr. Wall dated July 1, 1998, the response of Drs. Moral and Heat dated August 13, 1998, the preliminary report of Dr. D. V. Icedean and B.I. Clash dated August 18, 1998, and an additional letter from Drs. Moral and Heat dated October 21, 1998. I also reviewed the dissertation of Jeremy M. Artyr of April 25, 1996 and the grant application to the local foundation submitted October 16, 1996, by Drs. Moral and Heat. My determination is based on the written record and does not include interviews of other parties with the exception of my discussions with the Review Panel.

The Review Panel has concluded that an investigation of the allegation of plagiarism is warranted since Drs. Moral and Heat acknowledged placing sections of Dr. Artyr's thesis into the grant application without specifically acknowledging Dr. Artyr's thesis. In the preliminary stage of the investigation the Dean, through designation to Drs. Icedean and Clash, concluded that the complaints warrant no further investigation. Justification for this conclusion, with which I agree, is included in a letter from Drs. Icedean and Clash to me of August 18, 1998.

In my opinion, the Panel has provided no additional information although they have cited references from the literature. On the basis of the written facts, I believe that one could conclude that plagiarism, in a literal sense, had occurred although I am not convinced of this fact since there is a legitimate dispute over the issue of joint ownership of intellectual property in a collaborative project. The Panel report indicates that 'it is unclear to the Panel whether a thesis is the sole intellectual property of the student.'

If, however, one takes the most literal interpretation of plagiarism, I still do not conclude that this case represents a breach of ethics. At the worst, it may have represented a careless error with no intent to deceive others and no resultant *adverse effect on the research. Had there been intent to deceive, I do not believe Drs. Moral and Heat would have cited publications by Dr. Artyr on the same general subject. Furthermore, Dr. Artyr appears not to have objected since he has taken no action after being informed of the allegations.*

In view of the fact that the Panel has provided no new relevant information, I stand on my previous determination that there is no justification to proceed to a formal investigation, and the allegations are, therefore, dismissed.

Sincerely yours,

Dean A. Verage, M.D.
cc: Drs. Simon Wall
 Frank I. M. Moral
 Christian C. Heat
 Review Panel
 Bertha I. Clash
 Donald V. Icedean

Befitting his expectations, Simon knew that the exoneration of Moral and Heat of any wrong doing based on Verage's flimsy excuses had to be bad news for him. Even worse, the "Guidelines" offer no recourse; once the determination was made to dismiss the allegation, the accuser would be an open game.

James V. Shepherd

On a cool, breezy Friday, November 7, 1998, the FEDEX man rang the bell at the door to the huge old house surrounded by meticulously groomed large lawns and leafless trees on Shortest Avenue in Jefferson City. An attractive woman opened the door, signed on the FEDEX log for the big, heavy envelope, picked it up, thanked the man and closed the door. Mrs. Shepherd glanced at the label on the envelope that read:

> *From:*   *Dr. Simon Wall*
> *Anesthesiology Department*
> *Jefferson University*
> *Medical School*
> *Jefferson City, KS*
>
> *To:*   *Dr. James V. Shepherd*
> *President, Jefferson University*
> *1 Shortest Ave*
> *Jefferson City, KS*

When Dr. Shepherd came home that evening the big envelope was waiting for him with the rest of the mail on the small table at the entrance hall. He opened it and read the letter that was attached to a pile of paper documents.

November 6, 1998

Dear Dr. Shepherd:

First, I apologize for sending this package to your home address. I wanted to be sure that it reached you personally.

*Rather than describing the issue at hand with my own words, I have enclosed copies of letters, memos and literature describing in detail a case of **scientific misconduct** committed by two department chairmen at the Medical School. The copies are arranged in a chronological order.*

After you have read the enclosed documents and then the points I have listed below, I hope you will agree that your involvement in this issue is required.

44

1. *Is scientific misconduct, or even its appearance, less severe an infraction than any NCAA violation?[3]*

2. *One could realized from the enclosed copy of Dr. Icedean's letter to Dr. Verage that the office of the Dean has been less than enthusiastic in pursuing an inquiry into this matter. Verage's decision to dismiss the allegations of scientific misconduct (see a copy of his letter to Dr. Budsman, Ombudsman, November 4, 1998) was thus expected.*

3. *Dr. Moral's chairmanship is currently under review (5 year review). In consideration of the recommendation of the Ethics Review Panel to pursue a full investigation of scientific misconduct, I have suggested to the Chairman of Dr. Moral's Review Committee to postpone the review process until after the completion of the investigation. The Dean, finding no specific rules regarding such a case in the bylaws of the Medical School, decided to continue with the Chairman Review process. There is a good chance that the Review Committee will complete its task before the full investigation of the misconduct case is completed. How the Review Committee members can do their job, ignoring the information about the scientific misconduct, while they are aware of its existence or, conversely, how they can consider this information during the review process when the investigation is still underway?*

4. *There is much more to this case than what Drs. Moral and Heat will ever admit to, however, a full investigation should be able to expose most of it. Unless such an investigation is conducted, the university as a whole may suffer the consequences of not being completely forthcoming in admitting the existence of scientific misconduct and by rewarding the offender with renewal of chairmanship.*

5. *As a mentor of graduate students and a member of the thesis committee of others (I was a member of Dr. Jeremy M. Artyr's thesis committee, the thesis from which many sections were plagiarized by Drs. Moral and Heat), how can I assure future students that their intellectual property is protected at our university?*

6. *Interestingly, two students at the Neuroscience Department, one of whom is working under Dr. Moral's mentorship, were penalized recently for plagiarizing on course assignments.[4]*

7. *I have kept Dr. David O. K. Yesmam, Associate provost, informed about the case and provided him with copies of most of the correspondence. Nevertheless, I strongly believe that this is an issue of paramount importance of which you, as the President of our University, should also be informed about due to the potentially great damage that could come our way if the details of this case are exposed to the public prematurely, along with the fact that the offenders went unpunished.*

    I find it unacceptable that two chairmen in the Medical school who have been found to commit scientific misconduct will not be investigated and will continue to serve in their positions, setting "ethical" examples to future scientists and physicians.

    Since the Dean of the Medical School found no wrong with the conduct of the two chairmen, it leaves me no choice but to take my complaint to you.

    Our university is funded by the National Institutes of Health (NIH). Dr. Artyr's research and thus his thesis were funded by a NIH grant to Dr. L. Quarry. Plagiarism from Dr. Artyr's thesis is an NIH matter and of great public concern.

    I hope that by informing you about this unfortunate situation and by asking you to take action, I am doing what I feel is my duty i.e., assuring that our school will be the best place of learning it can be, free from misconduct of any kind.

    Please let me know your position on this case and what action(s), if any, you are planning to take. Based on your position and action(s) I shall decide whether or not to pursue this matter with the NIH and beyond.

    With best regards and great respect, I remain,

Sincerely yours,

Simon Wall, Ph.D.
Professor of Anesthesiology
cc: Dr. David O. K. Yesmam, Associate Provost

On November 12, 1998, Simon Wall received the following letter from Dr. Shepherd, dated November 10, 1998:

Dear Dr. Wall:

I acknowledge receipt of the materials that you sent me on November 6, 1998. I have referred the matter to Provost Caroline X. Pretty for her review and recommendation. She will be in touch with you as soon as she has completed this process.

Sincerely,

James V. Shepherd
Cc: Dr. Caroline X Pretty (w/attachments)
Dr. Dean A. Verage

By turning directly to the president of the university, Simon Wall aimed at killing two birds with one stone. First, he wanted to keep the case alive, which he succeeded as was evident from the President's letter to him. Second, he sought to hold the accused and their defender, the Dean of the Medical School, at bay. Or so he had hoped.

At 11:50 AM, on November 19, 1998, the telephone on Simon's desk rang. He picked up the receiver and heard Barry Truist's voice:

"Hey Simon, you have to hear this. At 7:30 this morning I was on my way to the monthly Medical Council meeting when, at the door to the meeting room I was approached by Christian Heat who, without any greetings, said that your complaint to the President regarding scientific misconduct could jeopardize both you and the department (Anesthesiology) as a whole. I told him that we live in a free country and that you are doing what you feel to be the right thing to do; that I cannot stop you from pursuing your own convictions and that you are not representing our department or anyone else except yourself. Then, Heat wondered loudly whether or not you have enough money in your bank account to get involved in a legal battle. I thought you needed to be aware of this encounter."

Simon Wall was speechless for a moment and then he thanked Dr. Truist for the information before hanging up. The next day he sent a memo to Dr. Truist detailing their telephone conversation of a day earlier and asked Dr. Triust to correct any inaccuracies and file the letter with his records.

Thus, it had become clear to Simon that his stone missed the second bird he sought to kill; the accused were not kept at bay. They were on the offensive after being informed by the Dean that the complaint was taken to the President of the University.

Notes

[3] In 1998, the President of JU was highly visible in representing the university in negotiations regarding NCAA sanctions against the university's basketball program.

[4] One of the students had to retake the course, while the other had to redo the assignment. In the wake of these two cases, the Neuroscience Department adopted the Graduate School Document on Ethics and instituted a rule by which each and every graduate student must sign that he/she has "read and understood the document's statements and also accept the Neuroscience Department's policy that documentation of plagiarism or cheating will likely results in his/her dismissal from the graduate program."

Hide and Seek

On December 3, 1998, Simon telephoned David Yesmam, Associate Provost, to inquire about the Provost's review of the complaint of scientific misconduct that was referred to her by the president. Yesmam, who was privy to the misconduct case from the time Simon filed his original complaint with the Medical School's Ombudsman, had assured him that he would keep him informed as to the Provost's actions. On January 6, 1999, after not hearing a word from Yesmam, Simon contacted him by e-mail:

Dear David:

Over 5 weeks ago I spoke with you on the phone regarding my complaint of scientific misconduct committed by Drs. F. I. M. Moral and C. C. Heat. I have referred the complaint to President Shepherd after the refusal of Dr. Dean A. Verage to open a full investigation of the case despite a recommendation by an Ethics Review Panel to do so. After the president referred the case to the Provost office I spoke with you and you assured me that you would keep me informed as to your office's actions, if any, regarding this case. I also advised you then that a journalist contacted me about the case and that I refused at that time to discuss the matter with him. Since I have not heard from you at all for the past 5 weeks, I assume that your office has no plans to pursue the issue. Please correct me if I am wrong. However, if this is the case, I will pursue this unacceptable scientific misconduct with the appropriate office at the NIH. I am sure that you agree with me that this is a very important issue. As a faculty member of this institute I believe that the only way to conduct scientific research is the honest way.

I do hope to receive a response from you sooner than later.

I wish you a happy and fruitful New Year.

Simon Wall

On that very day, Simon received a response from David Yesmam:

To: Simon Wall

From: David O.K. Yesmam

Subject: Scientific misconduct - Drs. Moral and Heat

It is now up to the individual student to pursue. I have spoken with him once and met with him - and will telephone him again soon. I intend to keep his actions confidential at this point, so I cannot report his actions to you or anyone else. I would hope that you would let him decide upon any action independently and at his own pace.

This was the first communication in writing that Simon received from the Provost's office. It became clear from Yesmam's response that the Provost's office decided to use delay tactics rather than investigate the case and make a recommendation to the President.

In essence, the Provost and her staff decided not to investigate a case of alleged misconduct when the complainant is a faculty member. However, if a complaint were to be filed by the student/victim of this misconduct, the office would entertain the possibility of opening such an investigation. Moreover, whether or not the student would take an action, this action would not be revealed to anyone. And a clear warning was also sent to Simon not to try to influence the student to take one action or another.

Thus, since two months had passed since the provost received the investigation assignment from the President, it was clear to Dr. Wall that such an investigation had never taken place. All along, the intention had been to vie for time with the hope that the whole case would be forgotten or that Simon would give up.

On February 13, 1999, after another month passed without any developments, Simon sent a letter to Dr. Shepherd, the President of JU.

Dear Dr. Shepherd:

Over three months ago I sent you materials concerning scientific misconduct (November 6, 1998). You responded in a letter (November 10, 1998) in which you informed me that you have referred the matter to Provost Caroline X. Pretty for her review and recommendation. You also added that she would be in touch with me as soon as she completed this process.

I wanted you to know that as of today I have not heard from the Provost. One cannot avoid the feeling that there is an attempt to let the issue fade away, although, I hope this is the wrong impression.

Would you please let me know whether the Provost's review of the matter has been completed and if so, what are her conclusions?

I also enclose a copy of the honorable congressman John Dingell's Shattuck Lecture[5] as several sections in his lecture are especially relevant (highlighted) to our case. I hope you will have the time to read it.

With much respect and best regards, I remain,

Sincerely yours,

Simon Wall

Simon Wall did not receive a response from the President to the above letter. On February 24, 1999, Simon sent an e-mail note to the Provost:

Dear Provost Pretty:

On November 10, 1998, President Shepherd sent me a letter in which he acknowledged receiving materials I sent him on November 6, 1998. The material concerns with my complaint to Dean Verage about scientific misconduct committed by two chairmen in the Medical School. The President said in his letter to me that you are to review the material and make a recommendation. He also said that you would be in touch with me as soon as you have completed this process.

I would appreciate your letting me know whether or not you have completed your review, and if you did, what is your recommendation.

I thank you in advance for your cooperation and consideration.

Sincerely yours,

Simon Wall

The above e-mail message remained unanswered. Thus, on March 4, 1999, Simon sent another message to the Provost:

Dear Provost Pretty:

On February 24, 1999, I sent you a note inquiring about your review of a scientific misconduct case at the Medical School. To my disappointment, as of today, I have received no response from you to that note.

I would appreciate your taking a minute to respond to my inquiry on this most important issue

Sincerely,

Simon Wall, Ph.D.

On March 5, 1999, Simon received the following e-mail note:

To:	*Simon Wall*
From:	*Caroline Pretty*
Re:	*Note of February 24, 1999*

I will have a letter out to you in the next couple of days.

The following day, March 6, 1999, at 11:07 AM, Simon sent a note to the provost:

Dear Provost Pretty:

Thank you for responding to my notes. Would you be kind enough to meet with me to discuss this utmost important topic? I know that you met with Dr. Jeremy M. Artyr several weeks ago and I am sure that you are familiar with the position of the Dean of the Medical School on this issue. It appears as if no one is interested in hearing about my motives, my views and possible suggestions and ideas to solve the problem.

Would you please consider scheduling an appointment with me as soon as possible?

I thank you for your time and patience.

Sincerely,

Simon Wall

At 2:00 PM that day, a telephone call came in from the provost's office and a meeting between Provost Caroline X. Pretty and Dr. Simon Wall was set for 4:30 PM that afternoon.

Simon was 10 minutes early to the meeting and was asked by a secretary to sit and wait in the hall outside the Provost's office. At 4:45 PM the secretary came out to apologize for the delay due to an unexpected visitor. At 4:55 PM, Provost Pretty stepped out of her office with the unexpected visitor, shook his hand and signaled Simon to step into her office.

Pretty, an attractive, trim woman in her 40s, flashed a quick, fake smile at him, invited him to sit in a chair across her desk and said:

"I am already late for another engagement, so we will have to do it quickly. I am ready to make my recommendation to the President. I spoke with the student who is not interested in pursuing the matter, so I do not see why the university should continue to deal with this case. I will recommend that the President adopt the decision of the Dean of the Medical School without any change."

Simon felt his blood pressure climbing. It had become very clear to him that he was the only one in the whole university who had any interest in investigating the matter and in finding the truth. The rest of the players all had been administrators, standing together, covering each other's back and doing their best to make this unpleasant case go away.

However, the fact that the provost agreed to meet with him rather than simply informing him in her e-mail note about her planned recommendation, expressed some indecision on her part. Simon asked her:

"Are you telling me that only the student can force you to investigate this case while I, a faculty member of this institution cannot complain against a peer of mine about his/her scientific misconduct?"

She thought for a moment and then replied:

"No. I am not saying that you cannot file a complaint. What I am saying is that the student is the victim here and if he has no problem with the issue, then, we do not have any problem either."

Simon could not believe his ears. Almost instinctively he shot back:

"So, unless a rape victim files a complaint with the police, an eye witness account of that very rape is not good enough for the police to investigate?"

Now it seems that her blood pressure started to go up.

"I did not mean it this way. I was saying that the student has no problem with the issue because Dr. Moral was his mentor and they worked together on the thesis," she was almost shouting.

Simon, trying to cool things down, said quietly:

"You realize that the student is in a very precarious situation. He is now a senior student in our medical school. He plans to continue here throughout his residency. If he is to file a complaint against two chairmen in the school he attends, what are his chances to be accepted to any of the residency programs in our school?"

She considered her answer for a moment and then said:

"Well, I still am going to recommend to the President to adopt the decision of the Dean of the Medical School."

Simon, by now completely exasperated, looked straight into her eyes and said: "Well, I respect your position and opinion on the issue. However, I am not satisfied that the university is doing the right thing by dismissing the case. I may have to consider my options."

She snapped: "What options?"

To which he responded: "There is a member of the House of Representatives Standing Committee on Science, Mr. Brown, who is investigating cases of scientific misconduct. One of them, very similar to the Artyr case here, involves a graduate student at Cornell University. That case received much attention both in the Ithaca press and nationally."[6]

Instantaneously, she snapped: "Don't you blackmail me, do you hear?"

Simon, now completely calm and composed, started to get out of the chair and said: "Oh, no. I am in no way trying to blackmail you. I am simply telling you that there are other options available to me to pursue this case. Here is another option. Myron R. E. Porter from The Jefferson City Times called me several weeks ago for a possible interview on the case. Although at the time I turned him down, I may change my mind. Anyhow, I want to thank you for your time and patience. I know that you have a busy schedule and I appreciate your giving me that much time at the end of a long day and a long week. Have a nice weekend."

He shook her hand, turned and left her office.

It was 5:30 PM and the university campus was almost deserted. "So," Simon thought, "they have decided not to investigate." If he did not continue to pursue it himself, the case would die a quiet death. Most disappointing was the revelation that the highest academic officer in the university, the provost, was unwilling to look into a possible misconduct case that could potentially cause the university great harm.

Moreover, it was clear that there had been no question in the provost's mind as to the fact that a scientific misconduct was committed. She did not, even once, argue during her meeting with Simon that Moral and Heat did no wrong.

He went back to his office, picked up the telephone receiver and dialed the number of Myron Porter, the science reporter for the Jefferson City Times. The reporter was already out for the day. He left his name and telephone number on the answering machine and hung up.

On March 10, 1999, Simon sent the following letter to Provost Pretty:

Dear Provost Pretty:

I would like to thank you for your time and patience in meeting me on March 6, 1999, on such a short notice following my request. In doing so you became the only administrator who has met with me to discuss the important issue of scientific misconduct, and I want you to know how much I appreciate it. Although, my feeling is that I was unable to change your mind regarding your forthcoming recommendation to President Shepherd on the Moral & Heat's scientific misconduct case, I respect your position and opinion on the issue.

There is only one point from our meeting that I would like to revisit. In no way did I intend or even think to 'blackmail' you (your choice of words) when during our discussion, and in response to your question, I mentioned that a member of the House of Representatives Standing Committee on Science is investigating a similar case of scientific misconduct at Cornell University. From the outset of my involvement in this case, the welfare of the Jefferson University has been my only concern, with much disregard to my personal welfare. Although my approach, as it turned out, was somewhat naïve, I honestly believed then, as I still believe now, that one must take a stand when one witnesses a wrong being done.

I look forward to working with you on more pleasant issues and projects in the future.

Sincerely yours

Simon Wall
Professor of Anesthesiology

Notes

[5] The Honorable John D. Dingell. Shattuck Lecture – Misconduct in Medical Research. *New Eng. J. Med.* **328**:1610

[6] Simon Wall was in contact for some time with a graduate student at Cornell University who accused one of her mentors of stealing her thesis ideas. The story appeared in Nature (**392**, 113, 1998) by Colin MacIlwain entitled "Congressman launches plagiarism inquiry" and another one, a year later, appeared in Science (**284**, 562, 1999) by Eliot Marshal entitled "Two former grad students sue over alleged misuse of ideas." Both pieces dealt with the same case of misconduct – Antonia Demas against David Levitsky & Cornell University.

Action, at Last, on All Fronts

On March 30, 1999, Simon Wall received a Confidential Interdepartmental Communication from President Shepherd. There was one unexplainable mystery about this communication; it was dated March 12, 1999. Clearly, the president wrote it only two days after Simon sent his letter to the Provost.

In a span of 20 days, from the day Simon's letter was sent to the Provost on March 10, 1999, and the date the President's communication was received on March 30, 1999, Simon had already agreed to and was interviewed by Myron R. E. Porter for the local daily newspaper, *The Jefferson City Times*. In his confidential interdepartmental communication, President Shepherd wrote:

Dear Dr. Wall:

This is in follow-up to your meeting on March 6, 1999, with Provost Caroline Pretty concerning your November 6, 1998, private correspondence to me in which you asked that I look into allegations of scientific misconduct on the part of two faculty members at the JU Medical School. On July 1, 1998, you reported similar allegations to Dr. George Budsman, the designated Medical School Ombudsman. Your initial report triggered the Medical School's prescribed procedures for handling allegations of unethical research activities. On November 4, 1998, those procedures were completed with a determination that there was not sufficient justification to proceed to a formal stage of investigation, and the allegations were dismissed. Because of your letter of November 6, 1998, I asked Provost Pretty to look into the circumstances surrounding your concerns.

Provost Pretty has recommended, in order to understand fully and clearly the positions of the persons involved in the issues you have raised, that I ask Vice President for Research, Nina Marshal, to appoint a subcommittee of the University Research Advisory Council to conduct an inquiry and to make recommendation to me. I accept the Provost's recommendation.

Once I receive the subcommittee's recommendation, I will then make a decision regarding the allegations in your November 6, 1998, letter.

This additional review beyond the official process already completed by the Medical School is an internal administrative matter. Accordingly, I remind you again that it is your continuing duty to maintain strict confidentiality.

Sincerely,

James Shepherd
cc: Caroline X. Pretty
   Dr. Dean A. Verage
   Dr. Nina Marshal,
   Dr. Frank I. M. Moral
   Dr. Christian C. Heat

From the President's letter one could deduce that the Provost, after having the entire weekend following the meeting with Simon Wall, to reevaluate her involvement in the case, had decided to return the task of investigating this case of scientific misconduct back to the President without any recommendation.

The President, who had no choice but to immediately devise an alternative plan, wrote his letter on March 12, 1998, but did not send it to Simon Wall until at least two weeks later, a time in which he probably carried out consultations with various people within the administration.

Considering that the President had in his possession all the documents related to the plagiarism case and that he could easily choose to stand behind the decision of the Dean of the Medical School, one could conclude several alternative conclusions:

a) *The President selected to appoint another team to investigate the matter since it was clear to him that a scientific misconduct by Drs. Moral and Heat did take place.*

b) *That the President and those in the administration with whom he had consulted did not feel comfortable with the dismissal of the case for the fear that Dr. Wall would expose their attempts at cover-up.*

The Provost, no doubt, warned President Shepherd of Simon's options, since the President, who in his letter claimed to remind Simon, **again**, about his duty to maintain strict confidentiality, actually had never done so.

Of course, any confidentiality at this point was a moot issue as Myron R.E. Porter from *The Jefferson City Times* was equipped with all the details of the case. Myron, after receiving a tip from an anonymous source, got all his information from the University itself under the Freedom of Information Act, which JU, as a State university, must abide by. Moreover, he had already interviewed Simon for a forthcoming article in his newspaper about the case.

Nevertheless, on April 3, 1999, Simon Wall received the following letter from Dr. Michael A. Walton:

Dr. Simon Wall
Anesthesiology Department

Dear Simon:

You may be aware that research space within the medical school and in the Princeton Institute for Infectious Disease Research specifically, is at the highest level of demand ever. With the expansion of research endeavors by investigators traditionally located in the Princeton Institute, the addition of new faculty members and external funding of new investigators, the situation has become even more pressing. Due to requests for space from several faculty members with no current assignments in the Princeton Institute, it has become necessary for us to critically review current space assignments. In some cases, these assignments have been formally made, in other cases current assignments are temporary, and finally some spaces are occupied that have never been formally assigned whatsoever. In order to approach these difficult issues in the most equitable fashion, I would like to request of you that within the next 15 days you provide me a summary on the accompanying page related to your research endeavors.

61

Precedence will be given to more senior, established investigators and to those with extramural, peer-reviewed funding. These data will be used to assess current space occupied by you and your research associates. Should you have any specific suggestions for arrangements that can be made to accommodate additional investigators, I would very much appreciate your thoughts and recommendations. I realize that these issues are of concern to all of us, and hope that they can be addressed to best accommodate the overall research needs of individual researchers and groups, as well as the Institute in its entirety.

Sincerely yours,

Michael A. Walton, M.D. Ph.D.
Assistant Professor, MedicneDepartment
Director, Princeton Institute for Infectious Disease Research.

The above letter demonstrated emphatically that the administration at the Medical School had not given up on punishing Simon with even stronger resolve. This letter also indicated that the President's letter to Simon dated March 12, 1999, although, received by Simon only on March 30, 1999, was also late being sent to the Dean of the Medical School, Dr. Dean A. Verage. If the Dean had received it earlier he would have acted earlier on arranging for the letter from Dr. Walton, as it was clear that Walton, a junior faculty member, had not acted on his own.

Thus, it took Verage only a few days to recruit the Chairman of the Medicine Department to devise a way to try to evict Simon from the rest of his research space. This space, two labs and a small office, is located on the second floor of the Westside Research Building. Most of the floor is occupied by the Princeton Institute for Infectious Disease Research. The Institute was established in the 1970s as part of the Medicine Department with funds from a foundation created by the Princeton family after the death of Dr. Princeton, a long time faculty member of the Medicine Department at JU.

The Anesthesiology Department occupied the two labs and the office space on the second floor of the Westside Research Building long before Simon Wall joined the department in 1982. Interestingly, among the research space assigned to the Princeton Institute there were three separate, large laboratories, two of which stood empty for at least two years and one that was used for storage of old file cabinets and useless equipment.

Thus, the Princeton Institute for Infectious Disease Research was not aching for space. Moreover, those very same empty labs in 1999 still stood empty five years later.

Upon reading Michael Walton's letter, Simon could not avoid reverting back to the threats Dr. Christian C. Heat made to Dr. Barry A. L. Truist, the Chairman of the Anesthesiology Department, regarding the damage that the whole department would suffer due to Dr. Wall's complaint. Simon never responded to Dr. Walton's letter and nothing came out of it, indicating, again, that it was simply a scare tactic on the part of the administration.

On Monday, April 6, 1999, the following headline appeared on the first page of *The Jefferson City Times*:

"JU faculty to investigate plagiarism charge in medical school: Professor claims department chairmen used student's thesis" by Myron R. E. Porter, Science reporter.

The reporter also interviewed other "players" for his article, including the two accused. Frank I. M. Moral claimed that the complaint was based on a grudge Dr. Wall held against him. Simon also learned from this article that Dr. Lidia Quarry filed a lawsuit against Dr. Moral, Dr. Verage, the Dean of the Medical School, and Jefferson University, "accusing them of creating a hostile working environment."

For the next two months, while everyone awaited the outcome of the investigation by the Internal Administrative Review Subcommittee (IARS) of the University Research Advisory Committee, Simon received a few e-mail messages and telephone calls of support. The majority of the faculty members of the Medical School, however, stayed away from the issue and never raised it in their meetings with him. However, a few criticized him for causing unnecessary harm to the image of the university.

The subcommittee investigating the complaint of unethical conduct of research took its work very seriously. Its five members interviewed many of the people involved in this saga, including Drs. Wall, Artyr, Moral and Heat. Drs. Moral and Heat were represented each by a

63

separate lawyer. Lidia Quarry refused to be interviewed due to her pending lawsuit against the university and some of its administrators.

Then, on June 9, 1999, Simon Wall received a letter from his long-time colleague and research collaborator, Dr. Ming U. Meek, from the Neuroscience Department:

Dear Simon:

As you know there is a change in the departmental political climate since the issue of plagiarism surfaced involving our chairman. It has been brought to my attention and to the attention of our graduate student, Jim Chang, by some faculty members of the department that your presence on his thesis committee may have an adverse effect on his thesis completion. This has resulted in an extensive soul searching for Jim and me. After considerable deliberation, we have reached the painful decision of bending to the 'political wind' of the department and to ask you to consider resigning from Mr. Chang's thesis committee.

We have known each other for nearly twenty years and I have always enjoyed your keen sense of scientific integrity and Jim has already benefited immensely from interacting with you in the past. I am certain that you will continue to positively influence this promising young colleague while he is in our graduate program and beyond.

With my sincere appreciation, I remain

Ming U. Meek, Ph.D.
Professor

On June 12, 1999, Simon responded to the above letter:

Dear Ming:

I received your letter of June 9, 1999 asking me to consider my resignation from Mr. Chang thesis committee.

Since my first and foremost concern is the welfare of the student who is under our mentorship, I would not hesitate to fulfill your request and resign from Mr. Chang's thesis committee as both you and he feel that such action will remove any adverse effect, real or imaginary, on the completion of his thesis.

Let me assure you that I fully understand the hardship involved in trying to resolve this conflict between your duties as a mentor and our collegial and cordial relationships. It is unfortunate that political considerations do influence academic and scientific decisions. Not less bothersome is the fact that there are several faculty members of your department who feel that my membership on Mr. Chang's thesis committee can in any way adversely affect his thesis completion. Will the decision to grant Mr. Chang his Ph.D. degree be a political one?

Notwithstanding, I herby resign from Mr. Chang's thesis committee.

I have no doubt that Jim will successfully complete his thesis and will be granted his Ph.D. degree. I wish him the best in his future endeavors and look forward to continuing our collaborative research projects.

With best regards, I remain

Sincerely yours,

Simon Wall, Ph.D.
Professor

Thus, new fronts had opened in the war against Simon Wall. To achieve results, Dr. Moral recruited his own departmental faculty members in an effort to push Wall out of any involvement in the affairs of the Neuroscience Department.

Applying pressure to remove Simon from thesis committees was only one approach. The secretaries in the departmental office were instructed to stop sending Simon notices about departmental seminars, a service that many faculty members in other departments subscribed for simply by placing their name on a mailing list. Simon's name was removed from this list as per Moral's instructions.

During the spring and summer of 1999, the Neuroscience Department was engaged in a highly active process of recruitment of new faculty members. One of the positions to be filled was that of Dr. Lidia Quarry who had been on a sick leave due to clinical depression.

Consequently, many candidates, as part of their interview with different faculty members during their visit at JU, also presented seminars. These were open to all who were interested. Simon, despite being "persona non grata" in these seminars, attended several of them, if and when the topic was of interest to him. Needless to say, all the candidates who were considered as prospects by the Neuroscience Department were well funded with federal grants, a prerequisite in today's business of science.

Simon attended, among others, a seminar by Dr. David S. Neaky from the University of California, San Francisco. Neaky presented an interesting seminar on his research, a presentation that was well organized and well received.

Two days later, Simon called Dr. Neaky's office, only to get his answering machine. He left a message for Neaky who called him back the next day.

"Dr. Neaky. How are you?" asked Simon.

"Dr. Wall, you wanted to share with me some information. Go ahead, shoot" said Neaky.

"Dr. Neaky, when you met with the different faculty members of the Neuroscience Department here in Jefferson City, did anyone mention to you the fact that Dr. Frank Moral is being investigated by the university for allegedly committing a scientific misconduct?" asked Simon.

"No! What are you talking about?" exclaimed Neaky.

"Well," Simon said, "I am the one who filed the complaint against Dr. Moral. He also used the research ideas of one of his faculty members to submit a grant proposal unbeknown to that member. The grant was approved and funded."

After a long moment of silence, Neaky sighed and then said:

"Well, this sounds unbelievable. Not that I doubt what you have just told me, but still, he is the chairman of the department. What does he have to gain from acts like these?"

Simon thought for a second and then said:

"Listen, you can learn more from an article that was published only two weeks ago in the local newspaper. I will mail you a copy and, after you read it, if you have any questions, do not hesitate to call me."

Dr. Neaky thanked Simon and just before he hung up he added:

"By the way, I also have an offer from the University of Chicago and I probably will take their offer, however, I have also promised Moral to come for a second visit to Jefferson City, therefore, we may meet again. Anyhow, thanks for the information" and he hung up.

Wall and Neaky were never to meet again, but their short-lived contact would play an enormous role in the academic life of Simon Wall for a long time to come.

Besides the misconduct case, other events took place at JU in the first half of 1999. Among them, the faculty members of the medical school had selected a new dean to replace the retiring Dr. Verage, a selection that was approved by the Board of Trustees. Dr. Jonathan S. Nobb was to assume his deanship on July 1, 1999, while Verage stayed on the job until the end of that year to assure smooth transition.

On July 20, 1999, unbeknown to Dr. Wall, the Chair of the Medical School Grievance Committee, Dr. Allan U. Griever, received the following letter:

Dear Dr. Griever:

We the undersigned faculty members of the Neuroscience Department are by this letter filing a formal grievance against Simon Wall, Ph.D., of the Anesthesiology Department. Dr. Wall has for several months engaged in activities that are detrimental to the well being of our department. His most recent actions are so egregious that we believe it warrants official sanction.

Our Department is currently negotiating with candidates to fill vacant faculty positions. We have evidence that Dr. Wall has

67

communicated with candidates for these positions subsequent to their visits to the Department. The nature of his interaction with them can only be interpreted as an attempt to sabotage our recruitment efforts. One of our candidates was concerned enough to inform us of Dr. Wall's activities. In this case, Dr. Wall sent a letter to the candidate using the Anesthesiology Department return address. He enclosed a note clearly indicating that he had an earlier telephone conversation with the candidate. Dr. Wall stated also that he enclosed a copy of The Jefferson City Times article dated April 6, 1999, outlining an allegation Dr. Wall had made against our Chairman. We are prepared to provide written evidence of Dr. Wall's activities.

We are outraged by Dr. Wall's unprofessional, uncolleagial (sic), and reprehensible behavior. His actions undermine the mission of our Department, the Medical School, and the University. Dr. Wall's unwelcome incursions into the affairs of our Department must cease. We believe also that Dr. Wall should be sanctioned for his actions. We ask the Grievance Committee to recommend that the Dean take vigorous action against Dr. Wall and that the Medical School institute other measures as necessary to prevent his interference with the business and mission of the department.

Sincerely,

Neuroscience Faculty
See attached sheet for signatures (15 signatures)
cc: Dr. Jonathan S. Nobb, Dean, Medical School
Dr. Caroline X. Pretty, Provost

Simon Wall found out about the filing of a grievance against him only on September 20, 1999, a full two months after it was filed. A colleague of Simon who was a member of the Grievance Committee brought it to his attention. It came up when that colleague asked Simon "are you planning to hire a lawyer or represent yourself?

Simon exclaimed: "A lawyer? What are you talking about?"

"In the grievance against you!" replied his colleague.

"What grievance?" Simon asked.

"Don't you know that the Neuroscience Department faculty members filed a grievance against you?" asked his colleague, and added: "You better call the secretary of the Grievance Committee immediately."

Still confused and in a state of complete surprise, Simon called the secretary that same day only to find out to his disgust that a grievance was really filed against him and the Committee's secretary failed to notify him and to provide him with a copy of that grievance as required by the Blue Book.

Simon found out later from his friend and colleague, Dr. Keath Wright, that the signature collection on the grievance against him was done at the end of a monthly faculty meeting of the Neuroscience Department when all members were sitting around the table and the Vice Chairman, Dr. Stewart P. Retender, asked them all to stay and sign their names on the grievance document.

Many among those who signed their names hardly knew Simon Wall. Other faculty members simply passed the sheet along without signing. Frank Moral was not present during the "signing ceremony," but his signature over this charade was undeniable. He had managed to turn the majority of his faculty members against Simon Wall even before the "verdict" on the misconduct case by the Internal Administrative Review Subcommittee (IARS) had been issued.

These faculty members, who themselves voted to punish graduate students caught plagiarizing, were evidently willing to assist their chairman to hide his misconduct from new faculty candidates.[7] Moreover, they were willing to punish anyone who would dare reveal to new candidates facts about the case.

Eventually, Dr. David S. Neaky reported to Frank Moral about his conversation with Simon and also provided him with the documents Simon mailed to him.

Simon could only wonder what motive Neaky had in reporting their communication to Moral. Nevertheless, Moral decided to take full advantage of this information in his fight against Simon Wall. However, since the IARS had not yet reached a decision on the misconduct case, he could not add his own name to the list of signatures on the grievance document, lest he would be blamed for retaliatory action against the whistleblower. The most he could do was to direct things behind the scenes.

For Simon Wall, grievance proceedings were an additional burden. This meant, among others, the expense of hiring an attorney and much wasted time, as he was sure nothing would come out of such proceedings.

There was one unknown in the mix, namely, the new dean, Dr. Nobb, who was working closely with Dr. Verage, the retiring dean. Verage had much disdain for Simon for sending the misconduct case to the president of the university in spite of Verage's decision to dismiss it.

The grievance letter was copied to both, the dean of the medical school and the university provost. This action by the grievants was contradictory to the spirit and intent of the grievance process. Involving the administration in this particular grievance case had been the real aim of Drs. Moral and Retender, not the resolution of disagreement between faculty members.

Simon attempted to arrange an appointment with the dean, but was rebuffed with the excuse that the dean's tight schedule prevented Dr. Nobb from meeting with him for the foreseeable future. It seemed strange to Simon that Nobb, who as an anesthesiologist was a member of Simon's department, would avoid meeting him.

Simon knew that the dean had already met with other members of the Anesthesiology Department, individually. Therefore, he tried again to arrange a meeting with the dean and sent him the following letter:

August 20, 1999
Dr. Jonathan S. Nobb
Dean,
Medical School

Dear Dr. Nobb:

Fifty days ago you officially became the Dean of our medical school. I know that the pressure on your time is enormous and fitting in an appointment with me, even a short one, is almost impossible. I tried twice in the past month to arrange for an appointment and each time your secretary told me that you prefer to postpone our meeting to a later date.

My interest in meeting you is not merely to introduce myself to you, as this can wait. I think that it is important for you to hear my side of the case of scientific misconduct against two departmental chairmen in our school. Undoubtedly, you did discuss this case with both of the accused and with Dr. Verage. I know that you have an interest in this case since you have inquired about me, so I was told. More importantly, your interest in the case must stem from the significant impact it could have on our school.

I hope that you reconsider your decision to postpone our meeting and allow me a few minutes of your valuable time.

I enclose a copy of my CV as a testimonial of my devotion to science, medical education and community service.

Sincerely yours

Simon Wall, Ph.D.
Professor of Anesthesiology

More than a year would pass before Simon was to meet the new dean under somewhat different circumstances.

Meanwhile, Simon had to prepare himself for two upcoming events, the expected recommendation of the IARS regarding the misconduct case and the grievance proceedings. As to the former, there was nothing he could do, except be ready for another dismissal of his allegations. For the latter, he had to document everything he could, confer with possible witnesses who, hopefully, would be willing to testify on his behalf and, of course, find a lawyer.

There had been one accusation in the Grievance complaint that he could refute easily. He was accused of *unwelcome incursions into the affairs of the Neuroscience Department.* It took Simon only 5 min to list those "unwelcome incursions."

Between 1985 and 1999, Simon served on seven graduate thesis committees (four doctoral and three master); presented two seminars in the department; co-authored with departmental faculty members 22 peer-reviewed papers, one book, five (5) book chapters, 27 abstracts and 10 grant proposals and interviewed more than 10 candidates for faculty positions in the Neuroscience Department in response to specific requests by Dr. Moral himself.

Simon was sure that the above-listed "incursions" could not be seen as "unwelcome." Two of his colleagues from that department, agreed to testify on his behalf, Drs. Keath H. Wright and Ming U. Meek.

Notes

[7] Back in February 1999, news about two Neuroscience graduate students who were caught plagiarizing and were punished, spread in the Medical School. Several other graduate students in that department complained about a new rule aimed at fighting plagiarism that was issued by the department. According to that rule graduate students were forced to sign a document stating: "I have read this document and understood that I can be expelled from the program if caught committing misconduct." Simon Wall, upon learning of the new rule, sent an open letter to all faculty members and graduate students in the Neuroscience Department. In his letter he detailed the basis for his complaint against Drs. Moral and Heat and provided copies of pages from the infamous grant proposal and their counterpart, identical pages, from Artyr's thesis. Thus, all members of the Neuroscience Department had an opportunity to see for themselves the documents on which Simon's complaint was based.

The Resolution

On August 28, 1999, the President of JU received a confidential report of the IARS:

Report of the Internal Administrative Review Subcommittee (IARS) Regarding the Allegation of Scientific Misconduct as committed by Drs. Frank I. M. Moral and Christian C. Heat

Background

The Internal Administrative Review Subcommittee (IARS) was appointed by Dr. Nina Marshal, Vice President for Research, from membership of the Advisory Council to serve as an advising body to President Shepherd regarding the allegation of scientific misconduct involving plagiarism against Dr. Frank I. M. Moral and Dr. Christian C. Heat by Dr. Simon Wall. Specifically,
Dr. Marshal gave the IARS the following charge:

- *To serve as an impartial group.*

- *To review the finding of a previous review of an allegation of scientific misconduct processed through a defined University process.*

- *To identify, through an interview process, any pertinent information not available during the previous review that could have impact on the original findings.*

- *To transmit to the President a review of the original findings, and any additional findings specifically addressing this allegation but not available during the original review.*

- *To make recommendation to the President, who will then make a decision regarding the allegation of scientific misconduct.*

The specific allegation that the IARS investigated is as follows: *"A grant application submitted to a local foundation by Drs. Moral and Heat contains 'many passages, paragraphs, and statements...[that] were copied verbatim from Dr. J. M.*

Artyr's thesis.' This constitutes misconduct in science that involves plagiarism."

The IARS obtained, reviewed, and considered information that was directly relevant to this allegation.

IARS Process

The IARS held an initial meeting to review the charge to the committee and to determine process. The IARS interpreted the charge as a request to review both the process and the findings of the earlier proceedings in the Medical School. In this regard, the IARS's role was **not** to make **independent** determination or whether the allegation had merit; instead, the task was to determine whether any grounds existed to disturb the determination made by the Medical School Dean, Dr. Dean A. Verage, as stated in his Novemver 4, 1998 letter to Dr. Budsman, Ombudsman of the Medical School.

After group deliberation, the IARS decided upon the following process:

- Review relevant documents related to the allegation and to findings related to the allegation provided to the IARS by Dr. Nina Marshal.

- Compile a list of individuals to be interviewed whose information was directly relevant to the allegation. The list included Dr. Jeremy Artyr, the members of Dr. Artyr's dissertation committee (Dr. Wall, professor in the Anesthesiology Department; Dr. Moral, professor and chairperson of the Neuroscience Department; Dr. Heat, professor and chairperson of the Neurology Department; Dr. Lidia Quarry, associate professor in the Neuroscience Department; and Dr Keath Wright, professor in the Neuroscience department) and Ms. Wendy S. Capegoat, Research Coordinator for Dr. Moral's lab where much of Dr. Artyr's dissertation research took place.[8] At the request of Dr. Moral, the IARS tentatively included four individuals on the interview list (Dr. Karine Kobbler, associate *professor in the Neuroscience Department; Dr. Lola I. Serve, professor in the Neuroscience Department; a research technologist in Dr. Moral's lab; a doctoral student in Dr. Moral's lab.) It was determined that the IARS would decide whether to interview these individuals after interviewing Dr. Moral and determining his reasons for requesting the interviews.*

- *Compile a list of questions for each individual to be interviewed based upon the information contained in the documents related to the allegation.*

- *Whole committee interviews with each individual.*

- *Review the documents and information from the interviews and determine the IARS's recommendation to the President regarding the allegation of scientific misconduct.*

Implementation of the Process

The IARS implemented the process as outlined above. The committee arranged interviews at the convenience of the interviewees. During the interviews, all interviewees were allowed the opportunity to provide any information and opinions and to contribute any additional documents that they believed were related to the allegation of plagiarism. All interviews were audio-taped for committee use.

Mr. C. Brad Justice, Assistant Attorney General from the Kansas Office of the Attorney general, served as legal advisor to the IARS on behalf of the University.

Prior to the interviews with Dr. Moral and Dr. Heat, a subgroup of the IARS and Mr. Justice met with Mr. Darin G. Framer and Mr. Rodney D. Fender (by phone), attorneys for Dr. Moral and Dr. Heat, respectively, to explain the interview process. Copies of the IARS's interview questions for Dr. Moral and Dr. Heat were provided to their attorneys. Both attorneys were present during the interviewing of their clients and provided opening remarks related to the allegation.

After interviewing Dr. Moral, the IARS decided to interview the four individuals (list above) that Dr. Moral requested be interviewed. The IARS wanted to ensure that we had collected the information and opinions that Dr. Moral believed were relevant and important in judging the validity of the allegation.

The IARS spent approximately 14 hours interviewing Wall, Artyr, Wright, Moral, Heat, the lab technologist and the doctoral student of Dr. Moral and Kobbler. It should be noted that the IARS was unable to interview Ms. Capegoat who is hospitalized with a brain tumor. (Dr. Moral stated during his interview that Ms. Capegoat put together the sections of the proposal that contained language common to Dr. Artyr's dissertation. Because of this, Ms. Capegoat could have provided key information to the IARS regarding the allegation; however her medical condition precluded this.[9] Also, Dr. Quarry declined to be interviewed by the committee.[10]

Findings

The IARS used the 'Guidelines and Resources Material for the Ethical Conduct and Reporting of Research at the Jefferson University Medical School' to guide deliberations. Specifically, the IARS attended to the definition of plagiarism in the reporting of research: 'reporting others' data without acknowledging the source' (p. 16). In addition, the IARS considered 'intent to deceive' as necessary to the substantiation of scientific misconduct.

Given the above guidelines, the testimony provided in the interviews, and the supporting documents, the IARS found the following:

Regarding the Medical School's definition of plagiarism ('reporting others' data without acknowledging the source'): With respect to Dr. Heat, the evidence clearly showed that he did not commit plagiarism. Dr. Heat did not contribute to the drafting of the grant proposal in question. Although he reviewed the proposal prior to submission, Dr. Heat testified *(and the IARS found no reason to doubt) that he did not recognize any similarity between the wording of the proposal and Dr. Artyr's dissertation.[11]*

In contrast, Dr. Moral oversaw the drafting of the grant proposal that contains sections of narrative that are identical to the narrative in Artyr's dissertation. With regard to this duplication, it is significant to note that the Medical School's definition of plagiarism is narrower than the definition that pertains in other disciplines. The Medical School forbids only use of someone else's 'data', not their mode of expression. Because the Medical School document controls in this case, the IARS used its definition of plagiarism to evaluate Dr. Moral's actions. Applying this definition, the IARS found no evidence that Dr. Moral used any 'data' belonging to Dr. Artyr in the grant proposal in question.

Regarding 'intent to deceive:' *Even if the IARS were to conclude (which it did not) that words in Dr. Artyr's thesis could be viewed as 'data' within the Medical School's definition of plagiarism, the IARS found no reason to question Dr. Verage's conclusion that neither Dr. Moral nor Dr. Heat committed plagiarism. With respect to Dr. Heat it is again conclusive that he did not contribute to the drafting of the proposal and, therefore, could not have copied the wording from Dr. Artyr's dissertation. With respect to Dr. Moral, he testified that the portion of the proposal in which identical language appeared were drafted by his research coordinator, Wendy S. Capegoat. Although no other witness had personal knowledge of how this particular proposal was written, several corroborated that Ms. Capegoat would often put together the first draft of background material of this sort. The IARS heard no evidence that suggests to the contrary. Moreover, Dr. Moral testified that he did not recognize the similarity in the language between the proposal and Dr. Artyr's thesis when he reviewed the proposal prior to submission.[12] Therefore, since there is no evidence that Dr. Moral or Dr. Heat recognized the parallel wording, the IARS found no intent to deceive.*

In essence, these findings support the conclusions that Dr. Verage stated in his letter to Dr. Budsman.[13]

Recommendation

Even though the IARS heard considerably more testimony than was presented previously during the Medical School's informal review process, the IARS found no evidence that shows either Dr. Moral or Dr. Heat committed plagiarism as defined by the Medical School guidelines. Given that the findings of the IARS are consistent with those of Dr. Verage, the IARS recommends that you do not disturb Dr. Verage's determination.[14]

Actually, Simon Wall did not see the final confidential report and its recommendation to the President until Dr. Shepherd himself sent him a copy with an attached letter on September 16, 1999:

Dear Dr. Wall:

The Internal Review Subcommittee has completed the review concerning your allegation of scientific misconduct involving plagiarism against Dr. Moral and Dr. Heat. The committee found no evidence that either committed plagiarism as defined by the Medical School Document. They have advised me not to disturb Dr. Verage's determination.

After reviewing the report, I have decided to accept the recommendation of the subcommittee. No testimony indicated either Dr. Moral or Heat prepared the draft of the section in question. The definition of plagiarism in the Medical School document is narrow and forbids use of data, not mode of expression. The evidence does not support intent to deceive. All of the above are relevant criteria in judging whether this instance of copying is misconduct in science.

The report does not address whether copying others' words without attribution is appropriate nor does it address whether authors are responsible for the content of their final products. I believe that copying is not appropriate and that authors are responsible for content. The Research Advisory Council is currently revising a university wide document on the ethical conduct of research, scholarship and creative activity.(15). The issues raised during the process of investigating your allegation are important to the academic integrity of JU and will influence the final product of their effort.

I appreciate your willingness to come forward with your concerns. The University has responded to your continuing concerns in good faith but it is now time to let this specific matter rest.

Sincerely,

James V. Shepherd

Two days later, The Jefferson City Times published the news with the headline:

"Professors cleared of plagiarism claim: JU pair's grant request had drawn fire."

And thus ended the official part of the University's investigation of this case of scientific misconduct. However, Simon Wall's problems had just begun.

Notes

[8] The IARS appeared to accept this claim by Dr. Moral, out of hand, a claim that was untrue.

[9] Dr. Moral's request from the IARS to interview Ms. Capegoat was a sham. At the time he has made this request he already knew that Ms. Capegoat could not testify. In an interview he gave to Myron R. E. Porter, The Jefferson City Times' reporter, in March 1999, he made the claim that Ms. Capegoat is the one who used Dr. Artyr's thesis to prepare the portions of the grant application that were similar to the thesis. Porter, upon finding out that Ms. Capegoat could neither speak nor recognize anyone, decided not to include in his article that claim of Moral. It is worth remembering that during the first investigation at the Medical School, Moral and Heat never made any claim regarding Ms. Capegoat's involvement. At that time, July 1998, Ms. Capegoat still possessed most of her faculties.

[10] Dr. Quarry had already filed a lawsuit against Moral, Verage and other officials of the University by the time the IARS conducted its interviews and had nothing to gain and much to lose by agreeing to be interviewed.

[11] Heat's argument of ignorance does not hold water. He served on Artyr's thesis committee only four months prior to the submission of the grant proposal. If he actually read the dissertation he had to recognize the similarities. It is more probable that he read neither.

[12] Dr. Moral's claim again makes no sense. If he was Artyr's principal mentor, as he had stated a year earlier in his letter to Icedean, the Vice Dean of the Medical School, then, he must have read Artyr's thesis at least twice or thrice, as Simon Wall did. If he did not recognize the similarities between the thesis and the grant proposal it could be that he never really reviewed the thesis since he was not the principal mentor, as he claimed. Rather, Dr. Quarry was the principal mentor and most of the work was done in her lab. Nonetheless, it appears that Moral did not tell the truth either during the first investigation at the Medical School when he openly admitted using the thesis in writing the grant proposal or when he testified to the IARS that he did not recognize the similarity between the two. This point also refutes the claim of the IARS that they were thorough and careful in their evaluation. They either did not recognize the contradiction between Moral's two statements or had chosen to ignore it.

[13] These findings in no way support Dean Verage's conclusions. Verage concluded that Artyr's thesis is not his sole intellectual property and based on this conclusion he dismissed the allegation of plagiarism. The IARS never even once dealt with the question of intellectual property.

[14] The IARS focused so much on the narrow Medical School's definition of plagiarism that they never once bothered either to check closely the grant proposal and the thesis to verify that 'data' were not copied or to ask any of the witnesses, and especially Dr. Wall, whether or not they were aware of any data that were copied. Of course, if they had asked Dr. Wall, he could have pointed to the table in the grant proposal that can definitely be described as 'data'. This very issue was, eventually, one of the strongest points Dr. Quarry brought in her lawsuit against Moral and others. Dr. Wall gave a deposition on Dr. Quarry's behalf confronting Dr. Moral and his university lawyers illustrating how Moral used data from Artyr's thesis to construct the table in the grant proposal. Shortly thereafter, the university settled with Dr. Quarry. The undisclosed sum of money Quarry was awarded is said to be in the seven-figure range.

[15] At present, five years after the Research Advisory Council started revising a university-wide document on the ethical conduct of research, scholarship and creative activity, no new document has been produced.

Direct and Collateral Damage

The first meeting of the Grievance Committee took place on October 20, 1999. It was convened mainly for procedural purposes. Joining the committee there was a hearing officer, usually a lawyer who is not a university employee, who helps sort out and, at times, decides on legal issues.

After all the procedures were explained to the grievants, who were represented by only two of the 15 whose signatures appeared on the grievance document, and to Simon Wall, the chair of the committee asked if there were any other issues needing to be discussed. Simon raised the point that grievances must be filed within 60 days of the occurrence of the condition complained about and that the grieving party learned about the condition on or about April 3, 1999. They filed their grievance on July 20, 1999, a total of 105 days after they first learned of the condition.

Dr. Retender, one of the grievants representatives and vice chair of the Neuroscience Department, claimed that they did not have all the information on April 3, and thus needed longer time to collect all the evidence they were now ready to present.

The Hearing Officer ruled in favor of the grievants and the meeting was adjourned. It was agreed that the next meeting would commence in November 1999. However, the November meeting did not materialize as the Hearing Officer, a candidate in the November elections for a Circuit Court judge in Jefferson City, won the elections and, obviously, could not serve anymore on the Grievance Committee.

It took more than a month to appoint a new Hearing Officer and to schedule another meeting, this time for December 23, 1999. In preparation for this meeting, Simon Wall sent the following letter to the Chairman of the Grievance Committee:

Dear Dr. Griever:

Now that the grievance proceedings against me are to restart due to the selection of a new Hearing Officer, I think it is necessary to revisit several issues concerning the filing and handling of this particular grievance.

1. **Informal Discussion** *(JU Blue Book, Article X.X.I): An informal discussion was never held between the grievants in this case and me, as required by the Blue Book. At no time was an attempt made to settle the case, again as required by the Blue Book.*

2. **Individual Recourse** *(JU Blue Book, Article X.X.IV.B): The grieving faculty members never sought to have the matter resolved through administrative channels and through consultation with the Faculty Grievance Officer as required by the Blue Book. "**The formal grievance was not filed within the 60 (sixty) days of the occurrence of the condition complained of, or within sixty days of the date the aggrieved party reasonably should have first learned of the condition.**" I have proof that the grieving party first learned about the condition on or about April 13, 1999. The grievance was filed on July 20, 1999, one hundred five (105) days or so after they first learned about the condition.*

3. *The official written statement of the grievance is addressed to the chairman of the Grievance Committee and copied to the Dean of the Medical School and to the Provost of the University. Based on information I received from the secretary of your committee, this is the only written grievance ever copied to officials within the university administration. The grievance process is designed to resolve differences among faculty members without the intervention of the administration. Moreover, the grieving party, without having all the facts in the case, already named the punitive measures they believe the Grievance Committee should recommend. These facts clearly indicate that the grieving party has no desire to resolve or to settle any of the issues. By copying the written grievance document to the Dean and the Provost they have attempted to influence these officials' opinion without first seeking a resolution through the Grievance Committee. By asking for sanctions and other vigorous actions against me they have indicated that they have no intent of resolving any of the issues.*

I strongly believe that each of the above points alone is a sufficient ground to dismiss this grievance case. This appears to be a clear case of harassment and retaliation.

Sincerely,

Simon Wall, Ph.D.

The administration involvement in the grievance process against Simon Wall was evident and was probably coordinated with both the Dean of the Medical School and the University Provost.

Sitting on a Delta Airlines flight from Jefferson City to Los Angeles on a beautiful morning, November 8, 1999, Simon Wall was scanning the program book for the upcoming Annual Meeting of The American Association of Neuroscientists (AAN). As usual, he was looking for names of friends and colleagues who contributed abstracts to the annual meeting.

The fast growing pace of the Association's annual meeting from 5,000 participants in the late 1970s to more than 20,000 in the late 1990s, did not deter long-time friends from looking for each other every year. Many are connected through mutual scientific interests, while others are acquainted through spending overlapping periods in the same laboratory during their postdoctoral research stints. All that one has to do is to open the program at the index pages, look for the familiar names and mark the program at the right place.

Simon was also looking for familiar names from JU. He found Lidia Quarry's name, although he knew she did not plan to attend the meeting, as she was too sick, suffering from stomach ulcers and depression. His friends, Keath Wright and Ming Meek, each were to present an abstract. There were three abstracts from Dr. Moral's group. One of the abstracts listed the name of Wendy Capegoat as one of the authors; an asterisk followed her name. An asterisk meant that the author is the sponsor of that abstract. A sponsor of an abstract that is submitted to the Annual Meeting of the AAN must be a member of the Association.

Moreover, a member cannot sponsor more than one abstract per meeting. A member who sponsors an abstract must sign his/her name at the appropriate place on the abstract form. Wendy's signature and her name with an asterisk on the abstract meant that she had read the abstract and had agreed with its content.

The deadline for submission of abstracts for 1999 annual meeting was May 1st of that year. Most scientists who submit an abstract to the Annual Meeting usually wait until the last minute before submission. Rarely is an abstract submitted weeks or months prior to the deadline.

Simon searched and found the two other abstracts from Moral's lab; the first included Dr. Christian C. Heat as a co-author and was sponsored by the first author, a postdoctoral fellow who worked in Dr. Moral's lab, the second sponsored by Moral himself.

As to Wendy S. Capegoat, she did attend a departmental social function in December 1998 with her husband James. She was sitting slumped in a wheel chair, unable to speak or to recognize anyone. She was completely immobile. It was safe to assume that the abstract form signed by her was not submitted prior to April 1999. The abstract forms are not sent out to all members before late January or early February.

Simon knew immediately that Wendy S. Capegoat could not have sponsored the abstract that carried her name. She could not have read it, she could not have comprehend it and she could not have signed her name on it. Simon felt ill as he thought of the possibility that at the time (March 1999) Frank I. M. Moral was explaining to Myron R. E. Porter, the reporter of The Jefferson City Times, that Wendy S. Capegoat was the person who prepared the draft of the grant proposal containing plagiarized sections of Artyr's thesis, he was either planning to or had already forged Wendy's signature on the abstract submitted to the Annual Meeting of the AAN.

The next morning, November 9, 1999, Simon entered the Business Office of the AAN on the 2nd floor of the Convention Center in downtown Los Angeles.

He removed his nametag that was pinned to his shirt just before entering the room and asked to speak to the Program Director.

Ms. Julie L. Swim graciously escorted him to her desk. As they sat down he explained to her that for now he preferred to remain anonymous and that he wanted to report to her a possible forgery of a sponsor's signature on an abstract to be presented in that year's meeting.

Julie was silent for, what appeared to be a long time, before saying:

"Well, I am not sure what you want me to do."

Simon thought for a moment and said:

"I suppose the AAN has rules about how to investigate a reported misconduct. I am sure that you keep the original abstract forms submitted for the Annual Meeting. You simply need to compare the signature of Wendy Capegoat on the abstract form from this year's meeting to her signature on the abstract she had sponsored for the annual meeting of 1997. If the two signatures are identical, you can simply forget about my report. However, if the two are not identical, I believe that the AAN should investigate, since its own rules may have been violated."

Julie said that she would bring Simons' report (she wrote down the abstract number and the name of Wendy S. Capegoat) to her superiors. Simon told her that he would drop in again in two or three days to check what she had found out. He thanked her, turned around and left the room.

Two days later Simon Wall checked with Julie Swim who told him that her superiors said that nothing could be done on the issue until all personnel is back at the permanent office in Washington, D.C. They agreed that Simon would call her four weeks later.

On December 14, 1999, Wendy S. Capegoat, Dr. Moral's loyal assistant, who decided to follow him from New Mexico to Kansas, passed away while sitting in her wheel chair at the sanitarium where she had spent the last six months of her life. Wendy never knew that her boss and friend blamed her for his scientific misconduct.

On December 16, 1999, Simon called Julie Swim and asked her what, if any, action the AAN was going to take in response to his complaint. Julie asked Simon if he could hold for a moment so she can transfer his call to the Executive Director of the Association, Ms. Nora Burgen. A few seconds later, Ms. Burgen was on the line and after Simon asked if the AAN was planning to take any action based on his complaint, she responded that the Association cannot act based on oral complaint. She said that any complaint must be submitted in writing.

Simon had a strong feeling that this was only an avoidance tactic. The assumption on Ms. Burgen's part was that since Simon kept his anonymity, he would hesitate to expose himself, something he would have to do once he submitted a written complaint.

Evidently, the AAN, similar to Jefferson University, would prefer not to deal with cases of misconduct.

Dumbfounded, Simon said goodbye to Ms. Burgen and hung up. After a few minutes of contemplation, he got up, stretched his hand to the top bookshelf above his computer desk and brought down the 1999 Abstract volume of the American Association of Neuroscientists Annual Meeting in Los Angeles, CA. Sitting back in his chair he opened the book on page viii, **Policy on Ethics.** It is one page that lists the policy of the Association on ethical conduct and publication of research. At the top it states:

It is expected that authors submitting papers or abstracts will have conducted their work in strict accordance with the following statement of ethics approved by the Association of American Neuroscientists in November 1990 and amended in November 1994.

Among others, the statement includes the following:

*...any questions raised about the execution of experiments or their **presentation** will be evaluated preliminary by the **Chair of the Program Committee** (in the case of an abstract), in consultation with the Chair of the Publication Committee and the Secretary of the Association. If possible, the matter may be resolved informally at this level. However, if deemed appropriate, **the matter will be referred to the institution where the scientific work in question was done**.*

Nothing in this policy hints as to the way by which questions about conduct should be raised, whether orally or in writing. Nevertheless, Simon had realized that unless a written complaint is submitted, nothing would be done. He decided to wait until after the New Year break to write his complaint.

The Grievance Committee met on the afternoon of December 23, 1999. This was a short meeting as everyone was ready to begin the Christmas holiday. The new Hearing Officer listened to Simon's argument that the time it took the grievants to submit their grievance document was longer than the 60-day period allowed by the Blue Book. Simon and the grievant representatives were asked to step out of the room and after a short discussion the Committee decided not to accept Simon's argument and hence to proceed with the grievance process.

The Committee was asked by the grievants' representatives to allow the addition of several names to the list of those who had signed the original grievance document. One of those who wanted to add his name to the list was Frank I. M. Moral. After he was cleared of all accusations of misconduct by the IARS, Frank wanted to join the retaliatory party that he had planned and put into motion.

The Committee deferred a decision on this issue to its next meeting. It was decided, however, that due to scheduling difficulties, the Grievance Committee would not resume the hearings until April of 2000. Simon was convinced that the whole process was directed by the administration and the aim had been to prolong as much as possible these proceedings, if for nothing else, then, to prolong the intended emotional torment of Simon.

A New Year, Same Old Song

On January 11, 2000, Simon, after a long soul searching, had decided to submit a written complaint to the American Association of Neuroscientists. He sent it to Ms. Burgen.

Ms. Nora Burgen
Executive Director
American Association of Neuroscientists
2020 View Point Circle, N.W.
Suite 555
Washington, D.C. 20046

Dear Ms. Burgen:

As per your request, I am sending this formal report to you on a possible case of misconduct by a member of the ANN.

In the Association's PROGRAM, 33rd ANNUAL MEETING, Los Angeles, CA, November 7–12, 1999, there appears on page xxx the Abstract #xxx.x entitled "xxxxxxxxx xxxxxx xxxxxx xxxxxxxxxxxx xxx xxxxxx xx xxxxx" by X.P. Xang, W. S. Capegoat and F.I.M. Moral, from Jefferson University Medical School.

Mrs. Wendy S. Capegoat, as indicated by the asterisk, is the author who sponsored this abstract, which appears in Amer. Assoc. Neuroscientists. Abst. 29: xxxx (1999). Sadly, Mrs. Capegoat passed away on December 14, 1999. She had suffered from brain tumor that incapacitated her for almost two years.

To the best of my knowledge, Mrs. Capegoat did not have the ability or the capacity to read, comprehend or sign the above abstract as a sponsoring author. Of the two other authors of the abstract, X.P. Xang is a research fellow who is not a member of the Association and F.I.M. Moral is Professor and Chairman of the Neuroscience Department and a member of the Association. Mrs. Capegoat was Dr. Moral's research assistant for many years and moved to Jefferson City from the State University of New Mexico when Dr. Moral assumed the chairmanship here in Jefferson City in 1987. The study reported in the abstract is Dr. Moral's and he is probably the one who signed Mrs. Capegoat's name on the abstract form and paid the abstract fee. I suspect that he is also the person who renewed Mrs. Capegoat's membership in the Association and paid her 1999 membership dues at the end of 1998.

Dr. Moral was investigated last year in a case of scientific misconduct (plagiarism). In his testimony to the investigative committee, Dr. Moral accused Mrs. Wendy Capegoat in that plagiarism. Needless to say, Mrs. Capegoat could not defend herself since she was unable to appear in front of the committee due to her illness. I have in my possession all the supporting documents, including a copy of the final report of the investigating committee, in case there is any need for them.

On November 9, I reported to Ms. Julie Swim about my suspicion regarding the possibility of Mrs. Capegoat's signature on the abstract form being forged.

I hope that this formal letter will enable you and the ANN to conduct a full investigation of this matter that, if proved to be true, is absolutely unacceptable.

Please let me know if I can be of any further assistance.

I would appreciate your letting me know of any action that you plan to take in dealing with this matter.

Sincerely yours,

Simon Wall, Ph.D.

On January 14, 2000, Simon Wall received by fax the following response from Ms. Burgen:

Dear Dr. Wall:

Thank you for contacting the American Association of Neuroscientists regarding the allegation of misconduct. Current Association protocol dictates that we are unable to retract any abstract or take any other actions, unless we hear directly from the university with an official letter indicating the misconduct.

If you were to contact the university and we were to receive an official notification of misconduct, we will follow the appropriate course of action.

Sincerely,

Nora Burgen
Executive Director

Trying to digest the meaning of this response, Simon read the letter again. *Current Association protocol dictates that we are unable to retract any abstract...unless we hear directly from the university.* Simon only asked the AAN to investigate, yet the letter speaks about an action that usually comes after an investigation, a retraction of the abstract. Did that mean that they had already compared the signatures of Wendy S. Capegoat on an abstract she had sponsored in 1997 with the signature on the 1999 abstract and found the two to be different? The answer is most probably yes. What appeared to be a real enigma is why the Association insisted that the university ask for such action based on indication of misconduct when Moral, by signing Wendy's name, actually violated the Association's rules, not those of the university.

The rule of sponsoring only one abstract is a rule of the AAN. The rule of sponsoring via a signature is also a rule of the AAN. Counterfeiting a signature on any document is a violation of the United States law, not just a scientific misconduct. Therefore, the only reason the AAN chose to speak about a nonexistent protocol must have been their unwillingness to bog down in a legal case from which they have nothing to gain, except, of course, enforcing their own rules and keeping misconduct out of their midst.

Simon called Ms. Burgen shortly after receiving her faxed response, hoping for a plausible explanation. Ms. Burgen explained to him that the

AAN could not afford to deal with cases like this one, due to, among others, the expense of employing attorneys.

As he was hanging up the phone, Simon tried to analyze the improbable thought that the American Association of Neuroscientists is willing to tolerate misconduct or even law-breaking behavior by one of its members for the sake of saving money.

Facing the unbelievable reality where institutions, large and small, are unwilling to fumigate the rot that eats them from the inside, Simon Wall turned to the last bastion of integrity he could think of, his colleagues at the local chapter of the American Association of Neuroscientists, the chapter he himself helped established ten years earlier.

After sharing with the President and four other officers of the chapter the information he had and the response he received from Ms. Burgen, they all agreed that it is the responsibility and the duty of the AAN to turn the information they have to the university and ask the university administration to deal with the case.

On February 22, 2000, Simon sent the following letter to Dr. James F. Edwin, the President of the AAN:

Dear Dr. Edwin:

It is with heavy heart and much hesitation that I am writing this letter to you. After much soul searching, many consultations with colleagues, and following on Ms. Burgen's advice, I have decided to turn to you.

From the enclosed copy of the report I sent to Ms. Burgen on January 11, 2000, you should be able to understand the gravity of the issue. This report was sent to Ms. Burgen after she had explained to me, during a telephone conversation, that the AAN could not take any action unless a formal report has been filed. It is important for you to understand that when I first approached Ms. Julie Swim in Los Angeles, I did it without revealing my identity, although, I said to Ms. Swim that I will not hesitate to reveal it if necessary.

Needless to say that upon receiving Ms. Burgen's response to my report (see attached copy of her letter to me of January 14, 2000) I had felt a bit exploited. After all, if my allegations are wrong, there is no need for a formal report from me or for Jefferson University to write an official letter indicating misconduct. Thus, I believe that the AAN has the proof for misconduct, but is not willing to act on it. I called Ms. Burgen on January 14, 2000, hoping to receive an explanation to her letter. She did explain to me that the AAN could not afford to deal with cases like this due to, among others, the expense of employing attorneys.

Nevertheless, I brought the issue to the attention of the officers of our local Chapter of the AAN. Upon their meeting at the beginning of February 2000, they agreed that if Dr. Moral broke the rules of the AAN, it is not the responsibility of Jefferson University to either enforce them or to rectify non-compliance. I do agree with their position and thus have decided to bring the issue to your attention.

Please advise me if you prefer to act on this case as the President of our Association or if you prefer for me to bring this issue up at the next business meeting during the annual meeting of the AAN as part of the agenda. I strongly believe that if the Association has chosen to enact rules not only in regard to abstract submission and authorship, but also for responsible conduct regarding scientific communication, it must be able to enforce them.

I would appreciate your immediate attention to this matter.

Sincerely yours,

Simon Wall, Ph.D.
Professor of Anesthesiology

C: Harry Moody, President, the Jefferson City Chapter of the American Association of Neuroscientists

Simon had to wait for a month before receiving a response from President Edwin.

March 22, 2000

Dear Dr. Wall:

Thank you for your letter of February 22 regarding possible improprieties on the part of a member of the Faculty of the Jefferson University.

I regret that you feel that your complaint to the American Association of Neuroscientists was not met with a satisfactory response.

As you know, the Association does its best to act diligently in response to requests from its members. Where issues of personal misconduct are conceived, however, it is not in a position to conduct investigations or make a determination that misconduct has occurred. There are potentially very serious legal issues involved in cases of this kind.

The AAN will publish retractions of abstracts if it can be informed that, as the result of an investigation by an official body, a determination of misconduct has been made. In most cases this will be formal notification from a University in which the misconduct occurred. As you point out, the Association also has guidelines covering misconduct in other areas.

I regret that we can do nothing about the case that you describe in your letter, without official notification from your University that charge of misconduct in relation to the specific abstract has been proven against the individual named.

I can understand that you will not be pleased about this decision. I will bring it to the attention of the Council of the AAN at its meeting in April. If Council decides that it wishes to pursue the matter further, I will be sure to let you know.

With best wishes,

Yours Sincerely,

James F. Edwin, M.D., Ph.D.
President

And thus, Simon hit another wall. Frank Moral broke the AAN rules, however, the Association insists that it is the duty of the university that employs Moral to enforce those rules. Moral counterfeited a signature of an AAN member, on an official ANN form yet, AAN officials claim that they have no power to enforce their own rules. The most perplexing of all was the ease by which good, honest scientists were willing to adopt their institution's administrative policy of avoidance.

Nevertheless, Simon could not afford to dwell on the AAN hand washing tactics when more then 50% of a departmental faculty membership was breathing down his neck with intentions full of malice and vengeance.

He could begin to understand how Lidia Quarry became so ill that her doctor ordered her to stay away from work for months and, eventually, never to return to her scientific career. Her own faculty members, directed and coordinated by Frank I. M. Moral, ganged up on her until they managed to break her, physically and mentally. They were reinforced with greater numbers now, united in their mission to save the good name of their department and chairman. They had a common enemy and they were all expecting their rewards, expressed as nice salary increases for all those who signed their names on the grievance document against Simon Wall.[16]

While Simon could only guess as to the depth of the administration's involvement in the grievance case against him, ominous signs indicated that this involvement had been substantial.

Simon knew that Frank Moral had managed to install several of his own faculty members in administrative positions inside the dean's office. His success in doing so was, in great part, due to the role he played in assuring Christian C. Heat's eventual selection as the Chairman of the Neurology Department.

No other position was more important and carried more weight than that of Dr. Lola I. Serve, a neuroscientist who was recruited by Frank Moral himself and who quickly climbed the promotional ladder. In 1996, she accepted a part time duty as Associate Dean for Faculty Affairs.

94

Within two years it became a full-time job at the Medical School and she has spent only a few days a month in her lab.

As an Associate Dean for Faculty Affairs, Dr. Serve had been in charge of faculty members' periodical reviews, promotion and tenure, and approval of request for Sabbatical leaves. Hence, she had played an influential role in the careers of many of her peers. Lola was also a witness on behalf of Dr. Moral during the investigation of allegation of scientific misconduct by the Administrative Review Subcommittee (IARS). She was the last to sign on the Grievance Document against Simon Wall.

Ironically, 1999 was the year Simon's five-year review took place, a process overseen and approved by Dr. Serve. She was also one of Dr. Verage's closest associates and, with Dr. J. S. Nobb taking over the deanship at the medical school she had become a very close associate of his, too.

She believed she owed Frank Moral much for her career success and was instrumental in assisting her benefactor in Dr. Quarry's case against him. In both Quarry's and Wall's cases Dr. Serve had a clear conflict of interest yet, she was not willing to remove herself from either of them.

Simon actually brought up the matter of her conflict of interest in the first and second meetings of the Grievance Committee. She had simply dismissed such claims by stating that she had asked the Vice Dean, Dr. D. V. Icedean, to take over the five-year review process of Dr. Wall as to avoid such conflict.

Upon finding that Lola I. Serve would remain on the list of grievants, Simon figured that both the outgoing and the incoming deans, Verage and Nobb, respectively, would be privy to all the privileged information that should stay within the Grievance Committee and with the people directly involved in the process. By the time the ordeal would end, Simon would have no doubts as to how deep the administration was involved in the grievance case against him.

Toward the end of February 2000, Simon learned that the Hearing Officer attached to the grievance committee had been replaced once again, and thus, the whole process would restart all over. By that time Simon had already hired an attorney, preparing for the possibility that he, as the whistleblower of the scientific misconduct case, would pay a high price and, thus, he felt he needed a legal advocate. The deep involvement of the administration in the grievance case made it a strong possibility that the process would be used to punish him despite the lack of any merit to the case itself.

A letter from Dean Nobb to Dr. Griever, the chairman of the Grievance Committee, indirectly indicated the Administration's desire to use the process to punish Simon. That letter was in response to Griever's submission of the grievance documents and correspondence to the dean asking him whether the case against Dr. Wall should proceed or be dismissed.

February 11, 2000
Alan U. Griever, M.D.
Chair, Faculty Grievance Committee
Medical School

Grievance - Members of Neuroscience Department Faculty vs. Simon Wall, Ph.D.

Dear Dr. Griever:

I have read and reviewed your submission of January 11, 2000, and the supporting documents and also had them reviewed by University Counsel's office. Based upon this review, it is appropriate for the normal grievance process to continue at this time, and I would ask that you proceed to consider whether there are sufficient grounds to accept this case for hearing.

The Blue Book states with specificity the procedures to be followed where there is a dispute within the unit. Each member of the Neuroscience Department Faculty who has grieved has alleged activity that, if true, would appear to me to be clearly "a hindrance to effective performance" as that term is used in Section X.X. IV.A of the Blue Book. Further, none of the exceptions with section X.X.IV or any other Section of the Blue Book appears to be applicable. Therefore, while unusual, these multiple complaints each appear to be appropriately resolved through the grievance procedures of Section X.X.IV.A of the Blue Book.

Thank you for your assistance.

Sincerely yours,

Jonathan S. Nobb, M.D.

Hence, the Dean of the Medical School had the opportunity to simply dismiss the grievance against Simon Wall and put an end to this charade. Considering that this Dean assumed his position after the misconduct investigation against Frank I. M. Moral and Christian C. Heat was completed, it is clear that he was "filled in" as to the history, the details and the players in that saga and was bent on continuing the Administration's crusade against Dr. Wall.

His letter would also explain the refusal of Nobb to meet with Simon back in August 1999 and demonstrated his familiarity with the grievance procedures and this specific grievance case.[17]

If the grievance process had been conducted properly, no one from the administration was supposed to be familiar with the grievance details until after the completion of its proceedings. Furthermore, the grievance policy had been enacted for the sole purpose of resolving disagreements among individual faculty members. The "class action" grievance that was launched against Simon by the members of the Neuroscience Department should never have been permitted to go forward as such. By all probability, Dean Nobb never asked the University Counsel's Office to review the supporting documents. If the Counsel's Office would done so, they would have alerted the dean that the "class action" grievance was against the rules of the Blue Book.

Thus, Simon decided to try once more to persuade the chair of the Grievance Committee to dismiss the case and wrote to him the following letter:

March 28, 2000

Dear Dr. Griever:

Now that the grievance proceedings against me are to restart for the third time with, yet again, a new Hearing Officer, I think it is absolutely necessary to deal with several paramount issues and questions concerning the filing and handling of this particular grievance.

97

First, I request that the Faculty Grievance Committee of the Medical School, due to the unusual nature of this "class action" grievance against me, address the following issues:

1. Can the committee unilaterally waive the **Blue Book** procedural requirement *[Sec. X.X.VI.A]* of having a grieving faculty member present in person **("the grievant shall first present in person and make an oral presentation...")**[18] and instead having a representative"? A basic aspect of the judicial system in the United States of America is that an accused person has the right to "face his/her accuser(s)." Thus, each grieving faculty member needs to appear and explain in person how he/she was "directly affected" {Sec. X.X.IV.B] by my actions (and see 3 below).

2. The **Blue Book** consistently refers to "**Individual Recourse; any faculty member; the faculty member; the grievant**" *[Secs. X.X.IV, X.X.VI.]*. Is there any precedent in the Medical school or in the University of a "class action" grievance by a majority of the faculty members of a department, including in this case, a faculty member who is an Associate Dean for Faculty Affairs? If not, the Unit Committee (Medical School) may wish to seek guidance from the **Blue Book** Committee and/or the University Grievance Committee.

3. Can the committee unilaterally waive the **Blue Book** **procedural** requirement *{sec. X.X.IV.A]* that states "**any faculty member directly affected by a condition believed to be unjust, inequitable or a hindrance to effective performance**," and instead only deal with how the operation of a department may have been affected, thereby, **indirectly** affecting the faculty member? Each individual faculty member should be required to explain specifically how his/her performance of research, teaching, and/or service was directly affected by my communication with a faculty candidate?

4. Can the committee unilaterally waive the 60-day requirement *[Sec. X.X.IV.B]* that states "**Any faculty**

member wishing to pursue a grievance through the formal grievance procedure shall file a written statement with the designated Hearing Officer within sixty days of the occurrence of the condition complained of or within sixty days of the date that the aggrieved party reasonably should have first learned of the condition." The aggrieved party learned about the condition on April 3, 1999 or even earlier. The written statement was filed on July 20, 1999, one hundred five (105) days after they first learned about the condition. Any action that occurred or that the grievants knew about more than sixty days prior to the submission of the grievance should not be admissible as grounds for the grievance. Sixty days is more than enough time for the affected grievants to "build" their case.

5. If a grievance by a group of faculty members is actually an accusation of unprofessional or unethical activity by another faculty member in the Medical School, should not said claim be considered by the Unit of the University Ethical Committee rather than the Grievance Committee?

6. Can a faculty member be a "surrogate" grievant for another faculty member (i.e., a chairperson or a full professor) who did not grieve under University Guidelines?[19]

*Some of the above points have been raised by me in a letter (December 23, 1999) to the committee, including the need for an informal discussion of an individual recourse as required by the **Blue Book**, but were not dealt with satisfactorily. The previous hearing officer ruled against informal discussions, comparing this grievance to a sexual harassment case where the harassed person cannot be expected to face his/her harasser.*

The following are additional points concerning the specific issues raised in the original written statement of the grievance that the committee should consider:

7. The recruitment of a faculty member in the Unit (Medical School) or the University is not a confidential process

*limited only to the recruiting department members. Candidates present seminars, visit different laboratories and have discussions with members of other departments. What is unprofessional or unethical about communicating with a candidate for a faculty position in another department? In this specific case, I have been involved in the faculty recruitment process of the Neuroscience Department for years as I was asked personally and specifically by Dr. Frank I. M. Moral, the Department Chairman, to participate in that process. I have interviewed scores of candidates for faculty positions in that department, some of which are currently faculty members. I was a member of six dissertation committees in the Neuroscience Department since 1986, the most recent one in 1999. I have served as a co-investigator on over ten research grants with faculty members of the department and have several pending grant applications in which faculty members of the Neuroscience Department are co-investigators. I have presented several seminars at the Neuroscience Department and have co-authored with faculty members of the department 20 peer-reviewed papers, four book chapters and 28 abstracts, and co-edited one book. Some of these collaborations are ongoing. I was asked by Dr. Retender to review a manuscript that was submitted for publication to a journal he was editing. When Dr. Moral considered hiring a technician who I knew personally, he sought my assessment of her professional capabilities. Based on my recommendation he hired her and on many occasions thereafter voiced to me his great satisfaction with that choice. Several years ago, as a confidant of Dr. Moral, he summoned me on more than one occasion seeking my input on various departmental issues. **Clearly, I have been, and still am involved in the academic affairs and mission of the Neuroscience Department.***

8. *The faculty candidate being recruited by the Neuroscience Department clearly stated in an e-mail note to Dr. Retender that his "encounter with Dr. Wall did not contribute to my decision not to come to Jefferson City" and that he "viewed*

this communication irrelevant to my recruitment." Thus, it is clear that my actions did not influence the outcome of this particular recruitment and no "harm" was done.

9. *This "class action" grievance was filed at the time when an Ad Hoc committee was investigating the case of scientific misconduct against the Chairman of the Neuroscience Department. That would have been the ideal time for informal discussion as required by the **Blue Book**. Both Dr. Frank Moral and I received a letter from President Shepherd in September 1999 stressing the need to put the matter to rest. A continuation of this "class action" could be viewed as "retaliation and retribution" against a whistleblower. The national Science Foundation defines misconduct as" (a) Fabrication, falsification, plagiarism, or other serious deviation from accepted practices in proposing, carrying out, or reporting results from activities funded by the National Science Foundation (NSF); or (b) **Retaliation of any kind against a person who reported or provided information about suspected or alleged misconduct and who has not acted in bad faith"** (K.A. Goldman and M.K. Fisher, "The constitutionality of the 'other serious deviation from accepted practices' clause," 37 Jurimetrics 149-166, 1997).*

I have also attached for your information a report from the November-December 1998 issue of ACADEME.[20]

I would appreciate your distributing this letter and attachment to all members of the Grievance Committee and our new Hearing Officer.

Sincerely,

Simon Wall, Ph.D.
Professor

This letter was sent only after Simon consulted with Dr. Garry A. Goodwill, an Associate Professor in the Bacteriology Department, and the only colleague in the entire Medical School who offered support and encouragement. As Simon's consultant, Dr. Goodwill was allowed to be present during the grievance proceedings with no other privileges, the same "privileges" that would be given to Simon's attorney.

The grievance process had resumed on March 31, 2000. As Simon stepped into the hearing room he was surprised to see Dr. Frank I. M. Moral among the members of the Neuroscience Department who were there. All those present were sitting around a large elliptical table. It just happened that Simon found himself facing Frank Moral across the table from him. As Simon looked around, he noticed that several grievants were missing.

The Chairman of the Grievance Committee announced that each grievant would have an opportunity to face Simon and voice his/her personal complaint and explain how Simon's communication with the candidate for a faculty position in their department had hindered his/her own performance. Then, Simon raised his hand and when recognized by the chair, he requested that Dr. Frank I. M. Moral be asked to leave the room since he was not one of the members who signed on the Grievance Document. Simon was looking straight at Moral as he made his request. He could see the anger creeping into Moral's face, the swelling of his neck veins, the total disgust and deep hatred that the man had for him.

Dr. Retender immediately protested, saying that as the Chairman of the Neuroscience Department and as a potential witness, Moral should be allowed to be present in the grievance proceedings.

Simon argued that in that case he would like for all his potential witnesses to be present during the proceedings. A decision had to be made on Simon's request by the committee.

To allow undisturbed deliberations by the committee members, Simon and the grievants were asked to step out of the room. Ten minutes later everyone were called back in. Once again as they sat, the chairman of the committee announced that their decision had been to ask Dr. Moral to leave since he was not one of those who signed on the grievance document. All eyes were on Frank Moral as he slowly got out of his chair, his expression that of a beaten puppy, and walked out of the room.

The next three hours were spent listening to only two grievants and to Simon who had the chance only to question one of them. It was shortly after 12:00 noon. The meeting was stopped and a new date for continuation was set for late April of 2000.

By Simon's calculations, at the current pace of statements and questioning, the grievance proceedings could stretch into the next year.

Nonetheless, two days after the hearing of March 31, 2000, Garry Goodwill, Simon's consultant, called and suggested to put an end to the fiasco by offering an apology to the grieving members of the Neuroscience Department. Simon thought for a while about the idea. He considered the time and aggravation that could be saved if such an apology were offered and decided to give it a try, although, deep inside he had the feeling that neither Frank Moral nor the Dean would be satisfied with a mere apology. On April 1, 2000, Simon Wall sent the following letter to the Chairman of the Grievance Committee and also faxed it to Dr. S. P. Retender.

Dear Dr. Griever:

Realizing that the grievance case brought up against me by the members of the Neuroscience Department will continue to consume valuable time of all those involved in these proceedings, I have decided to offer the following:

I am ready to officially apologize to the grievants for what they perceived as an interference with their departmental affairs. In return for my apology, the grievants will agree to withdraw their grievance.

If and when I shall hear from you of such an agreement, I will immediately issue an official letter of apology.

Please share this letter with all members of the Grievance Committee and the Hearing Officer.

Sincerely,

Simon Wall, Ph.D
Professor

On April 14, 2000, the secretary of the grievance Committee forwarded to Simon an e-mail note that was sent to the committee by Dr. S. P. Retender on April 9, 2000.

> *Dr. Wall FAXed to me a copy of his proposed "apology." It is insulting, arrogant in tone, and completely unacceptable. Clearly, we shall need to continue the hearing. Before we reconvene, however, there are a few points that need clarification. It seems that the hiatus in the hearing should enable the committee to make some decisions on several of the procedural issues raised earlier. These issues were simply postponed to allow us to proceed at our initial foray into March 31. We should like to know the Committee's opinion concerning the following before we proceed.*
>
> *1. I believe that the grievance signed by several faculty members represents the signers and that if any are unable to attend the hearing, all should remain instruments of the grievance. The Department is its faculty; Dr. Wall's interference with departmental affairs by definition affects the faculty. The signers' complaints are given in the grievance letter dated July 9, 1999, and their concerns for issues raised there are valid under any circumstances.*
>
> *2. May Dr. Moral be included among those filing the grievance?*
>
> *Finally, I should like to notify the Committee that we reserve the right to call the following witnesses: Dr. Frank I. M. Moral (if not permitted to participate as a grievant) and Dr. David S. Neaky (possibly by videoconference).[21]*
>
> *Sincerely,*
>
> *Dr. Stewart P. Retender*

As Simon glared at his computer screen and mumbled to himself "so much for apologizing," he could not help himself but to take an account of the past 22 months since Lidia Quarry stepped into his office with the infamous grant proposal in her hand.

Although 1998 was, research-wise, a productive year for him, not much happened through 1999, since most of his time and mind were wrapped in both the misconduct investigation and the grievance case against him.

Thus, it appeared as if the price for fulfilling one's duty had continued to climb. Over the months of April, May and June of 2000, the grievance proceedings consumed over 20 hours of hearings and many more in preparations.

Simon's attorney sat throughout those hearings and her bill reached $3,000 and was growing. The members of the Grievance Committee themselves appeared to grow tired of the process as they continued to listen to unsubstantiated claims by faculty members that somehow all of them had lost so much upon Neaky's decision not to join their department.

The impression was that their careers were badly damaged by Neaky's decision and they blamed it all on Simon, who, somehow, managed to persuade Neaky not to come to Jefferson City. And that, despite the fact that Neaky himself specifically stated in his e-mail message to Moral that his decision not to come to Jefferson City had nothing to do with his communication with Simon.

The identical arguments used by each of the grievants in their attempt to demonstrate how Simon's actions affected their personal careers strongly suggest that they were all coached, prepared and rehearsed for their presentations to the Grievance Committee.

Nonetheless, each grievant attempted to persuade the committee members that Neaky would have joined their department if not for Simon's interference. Frank Moral was not allowed to join the rest of his grieving faculty members. However, he was allowed to appear as a witness on their behalf. By June 2000, Simon had managed to make the misconduct allegation against Frank I. M. Moral the central issue in the grievance proceedings as one grievant after another, in response to his relentless and persistent questioning, admitted that if they had the type of information Simon had at the time he communicated with Dr. David S. Sneaky, they, too, would have considered sending a warning about a recruiting chairman who had been accused of plagiarism. While some grievants admitted that they would issue such a warning only to a family member or a very close friend, others simply remained silent, especially when Simon distributed copies of the grant proposal with highlighted paragraphs along with copies of the identical paragraphs in Dr. Artyr's doctoral dissertation.

As Frank Moral was anxiously awaiting his turn to step into the hearing room and throw the last punch that would send Simon falling to the canvas, his own conspirators had realized that once they allowed their chief to sit in the witness chair, he would be an open game for Simon and his questioning. The plagiarism issue would become the central issue, and with Moral's infamous short temper, things could be said in response to provocation that would do more harm than had already been done.

Thus, on the Committee's one next-to-last meeting, the grieving faculty members of the Neuroscience Department came back after a break and announced that they had no more witnesses to present.

Consequently, Dr. Frank I. M. Moral, Chairman, Neuroscience Department, Medical School, Jefferson University, was denied the one desire that consumed him for months, namely, to personally contribute to the demise of his accuser.

The last meeting of the Faculty Grievance Committee of the Medical School took place in mid-June 2000.

Simon called five witnesses, two of them from the Neuroscience Department, who, when asked why they did not join the others in signing the grievance document, responded by declaring that it was clear to them from the outset that the sole purpose of the mass signing and filing a grievance against Dr. Wall was a sham aimed solely at punishing Simon for his whistle blowing.

They added that to the best of their knowledge other faculty members did not sign their names on the grievance document for similar reasons. Two other professors volunteered to appear on Simon's behalf since for them, after learning about the grievance proceeding, it was clear that this whole show was intended solely for retaliation. The witnesses scolded all the grievants for participating in such a sham, but kept their harshest remarks for the members of Grievance Committee and its Chairman for allowing the process to take place.

The last witness on Simon's list was President Shepherd. Simon sent to Dr. Shepherd a letter asking him to testify on his behalf.

May 28, 2000

Dr. James V. Shepherd
President, JU.

Dear Dr. Shepherd:

I do have an unusual request of you that I hope you would be able to fulfill.

I am involved in grievance proceedings against me by members of the Neuroscience Department. They claim that I interfered with their departmental affairs by contacting a faculty candidate of their department in March 1999, providing him with information regarding the allegations against Dr. Frank Moral's scientific misconduct.

In the April 17, 1999 issue of the Jefferson University student newspaper, The Jeffersonian, you were quoted saying, in response to a letter sent by Dr. Allen Johansson to an Art & Science Deanship candidate, as follows.[22]

"It is unfortunate that some members of our academic community are evidently dissatisfied or even disgruntled about the University, but that is a normal part of life of any university."

Would you be willing to testify in the above-mentioned grievance proceedings as to your standing on this issue? If your schedule does not permit you to appear as a witness, would you be willing to submit a document corroborating that the above quote represents your position on the issue?

I would greatly appreciate your consideration and understanding.

Sincerely yours,

Simon Wall, Ph.D.

Although Shepherd refused to appear in person, he sent a short note to Simon confirming that what was written in the student newspaper is accurate and does represent his views and that Simon can use it as evidence. Thus, Simon introduced Dr. Shepherd's note to him and a copy of the specific issue of the Jeffersonian newspaper that carried the story and the quotes of both Shepherd and Johansson as evidence.

The committee asked Dr. Retender whether or not he had anything else he would like to add as the representative of the grievants. Retender took his time before saying: "Yes, I believe that my colleagues and I have clearly proved our original claim that Dr. Wall interfered in the affairs of our department. We feel that his actions cannot go unpunished. Thus, we ask the committee to formally reprimand Dr. Wall for his unprofessional and unethical behavior. We also believe that reprimand alone is insufficient and he should be used to set an example so that similar behavior will not occur again. We believe that the most fitting punishment would be for the University to withhold three months of his salary."

Simon was offered an equal opportunity for a summary, but he declined. This ended the last hearing of the Grievance Committee.

On July 1, 2000 the committee sent the following report to Dr. J. S. Nobb, the Dean of the Medical School:

Dear Dr. Nobb:

Following a careful and lengthy deliberation and working within the parameters established by the Blue Book Procedural Code X.X.IV.A, it is the unanimous opinion of the faculty grievance committee that all of the grievants complaints against Dr. Wall be dismissed.

The committee conducted a pre-hearing on March 31 and initial hearing on April 26, 2000 with additional hearings on June 9th and June 16th, to complete the review process.

The complaint of the grievant, Dr. Moral, was dismissed because of failure to comply with limitations period. Ten grievants gave testimony. Four witnesses gave testimony on behalf of Dr. Wall who was represented by legal counsel, Ms.

Patricia Jewel. The grievants were informed that according to the Blue Book procedural requirement X.X.IV.A, they were required to provide evidence that Dr. Wall's alleged actions had resulted in a condition that had been a hindrance to their effective performance as faculty members.

The following effects were identified:

- *Loss of potential research collaboration with Dr. Neaky noted by four grievants.*

- *No specific projects had been initiated but Dr. Neaky's potential to assist with research initiatives in the department was frequently cited.*

- *Loss of Dr. Neaky as a potential resource for assisting graduate students which was noted by Dr. Serve, Associate Dean for Faculty Affairs.*

- *Loss of resources provided by potential external grants of Dr. Neaky, particularly noted by Dr. Retender.*

- *The loss of Dr. Neaky resulted in extra teaching load for three faculty members.*

- *The loss of Dr. Neaky's ability to provide assistance with some specialized departmental equipment was noted by three grievants. It was also pointed out that this equipment has been in the department for approximately four years and it appeared there were others who could assist with acquiring the skills to use it.*

- *General effects on departmental morale noted by two grievants.*

- *Loss of faculty time in counter-acting the actions of Dr. Wall noted by Dr. Serve.*

- *General effect on the entire departmental team noted by four grievants.*

It was the consensus of the committee that the above examples in some instances would have increased the workload and interfered with the potential to collaborate in the future. However, they did not exceed the threshold of causing a significant hindrance to performance as faculty members, especially since most of the above effects were predicated on the allegation that the actions of Dr. Wall had resulted in the loss of Dr. Neaky as a faculty member. Yet, as part of the evidence, the e-mail from Dr. Neaky states "my encounter with Dr. Wall did not contribute to my decision not to come to Jefferson City." The committee accepted that statement as fact and therefore felt that the grievants were unable to provide convincing evidence that Dr. Wall's actions had resulted in Dr. Neaky not coming to Jefferson University.

Given that the committee worked within the parameters as outlined in the Blue Book as previously noted, some of the concerns about Dr. Wall's behavior did not fall within this narrow definition and therefore could not be addressed.

In summary, the grievants failed to show that Dr. Wall's actions resulted in the failure to recruit Dr. Neaky or significantly hindered performance as faculty members.

Sincerely,

Faculty Grievance Committee, Medical School.

On July 15, 2000, just before driving to the airport to catch a flight that would take him overseas for 10 days, Simon called the Committee's secretary to find out whether or not the Dean had accepted the findings and recommendation of the Grievance Committee. She informed Simon that as of that moment no word had been heard from the dean.

According to the Blue Book the Dean has 15 days from the date he/she receives the committee's report to make a decision and must convey it in writing to the grievants, the person against whom the grievance was directed, and the committee. Simon went on his trip without knowing the final outcome of the case against him.

He had to wait another month following his return to the country before receiving a copy of a letter from Dean Nobb to the Chairman of the Grievance Committee, Dr. Griever.

August 26, 2000

Dear Dr. Griever:

I am in receipt of your letters of July 1, 2000, and August 12, 2000, which contained the opinion of the Grievance Committee in the grievance of Retender et al. versus Wall. I accept the Committee's opinion that within the narrow definition used by the committee, this grievance be dismissed.

I do, however, find Dr. Wall's actions inappropriate and potentially damaging to the Neuroscience Department. Based on this finding, I direct Dr. Wall that such inappropriate actions should cease.

Sincerely yours,

Jonathan S .Nobb, M.D.
Dean, Medical School

Simon wondered why it took the dean almost two months to approve the committee's findings and opinion. In doing so, Dr. Nobb also ignored the strict timeline allowance as stated by the Blue Book. Only after reading the letter for the second time had Simon recognized the fact that there was a second letter from the Grievance Committee to the Dean dated August 12, 2000. Simon had no clue as to the content of this second letter or the reason for it. One could only speculate that a continued communication between the Dean and the Committee went on past July 1, 2000, the date the Committee' report was issued.

Simon picked up the phone and dialed Dr. Tina Chancey's number. As a member of the Grievance Committee she appeared to be impartial during the long hours of the hearings of Simon's case and remained silent most of the time. Simon simply asked her if she would be willing to explain to him the mystery behind the second letter the Committee sent to the Dean. Tina sounded a bit surprised as she asked Simon: "Don't you know about the Dean's letter to us?"

Simon, hesitantly, asked: "What letter?"

Tina replied by asking him to drop by her office while she prepared copies of the Dean's letter and the Committee's response to it. Simon picked up the copies, thanked Tina, returned to his office, sat at his desk and began reading.

July 16, 2000

Dr. Alan U. Griever
Chairman, Medical School Grievance Committee

Dear Dr. Griever:
Re: Retender et al. vs Wall

I am in receipt of your letter dated July 1, 2000, containing the opinion of the Grievance Committee in the above referenced grievance, and have reviewed both the conclusions of the Committee and the underlying file material. Based upon this review, I am concerned that your review has been too narrow. While the Committee correctly determined that its obligations were to determine if Dr. Wall's actions had resulted in hindrance to effective performance of the duties of any of the grievants, I am concerned with the Committee's statement that Dr. Wall's actions did not exceed the threshold of causing a significant hindrance to performance of faculty members in the Neuroscience Department.

Interference with another department's internal operations might affect individuals in that department adversely (and hence, be a hindrance to effective performance) regardless of whether any given individual accepts a faculty appointment and regardless of whether or not such interference caused the decision to decline the appointment. The issue that the committee should address is whether Dr. Wall's interference, regardless of whether it was successful, could reasonably be concluded to have had a negative effect such that it was a hindrance to the effective performance of the duties of any grievant.

Therefore, I am returning this matter to the Committee with the request that it broaden the scope of its review to determine, in this broader context, whether Dr. Wall engaged in inappropriate behavior which hindered the effective performance of the duties of any grievant. The act of interference may constitute action that may appropriately be grieved, and I request the Committee to review this case, in such a manner as deems appropriate, to determine if that situation exists for any of these grievants.

Thank you for your cooperation in this matter.

Sincerely,

Jonathan S. Nobb

Simon finished reading, took a deep breath and closed his eyes. As is the case with most of us, Simon was hoping that, despite the many warnings friends and colleagues sent his way, fairness would prevail within the academic community and, especially, within his own university. Thus, he had chosen to ignore all the warnings about standing up to the administration. He was told that although, many administrators are ex-scientists, it does not make any difference; once a scientist crosses the divide and joins the administration camp, the changes are quick and permanent. The goals, the rewards, the standards of administrators, all are different from those of scientists.

Thus, while the plagiarist administrator (Dr. Frank I. M. Moral, Chairman, Neuroscience Department) was given the benefit of the doubt by applying in his case the narrower possible definition of plagiarism ("*data, not words*"), for the scientist whistleblower (Dr. Simon Wall, Anesthesiology Department), the broader definitions of hindrance of another colleague's performance must be applied.

On August 12, 2000, the Chairman of the Grievance Committee sent his reply to the Dean's request.

Dr. Jonathan S. Nobb
Dean, Medical School

   Re: Grievance Neuroscience Faculty vs. Simon Wall, Ph.D.

Dear Dr. Nobb:

The Faculty grievance Committee met on August 2, 2000, in response to your letter of July 16, 2000. The consensus of the committee was that our work had been completed with the production of the report submitted to you dated July 1, 2000, and disseminated simultaneously to both the grievants and the defendant as per Blue Book X.X.X.A.

The committee is satisfied given the extensive and lengthy nature of the hearing process that Dr. Wall's actions failed to reach a level that resulted in a hindrance to the effective performance of any grievant.

Sincerely,

Alan U. Griever, M.D.
Chairman, Medical School
Faculty Grievance Committee

Seeing this response of Dr. Griever to Dean Nobb gave Simon a glimpse of hope that not everything is lost. It seemed that the members of the Grievance Committee themselves had realized that the whole process was orchestrated by the administration and the committee simply became an instrument of retaliation against a whistleblower.

Shortly thereafter, Dr. Griever, the Chairman of the Grievance Committee, requested from Dr. Nobb, the Dean of the Medical School, to be replaced. His official explanation for the request was the great demand his duties as the chairman of the committee had on his time. However, in a conversation with Simon almost a year later, Dr. Griever admitted that the real reason for his resignation was the bad taste he and several other members of the committee had due to the unacceptable interference by the administration in the committee's affairs.

Simon found it ironic that he, the whistleblower, was to be punished for supposedly interfering in the affairs of another department, while the administration did not hesitate to interfere in the affairs of an independent faculty committee in an attempt to influence the committee's decision.

Notes

[16] Since 1989, when all chairpersons became administrators at JU, they had much greater power in deciding the percentage of salary increase any given faculty member received. In 2000, all faculty members of the Neuroscience Department who signed their names on the grievance document against Dr. Simon Wall received higher percentage increase in their salary than faculty members who did not sign. Dr. S. P. Retender, who led the campaign against Dr. Lidia Quarry and later against Simon Wall, was rewarded handsomely both in 1999 and in 2000 with 6% increase in each of these years. The average increase at the University was 3%. Due to many complaints, this subjective practice was changed. All Medical School departments are now required to have a Salary Increase Based on Performance (SIBOP) Document that defines specifically how salary increases are determined based on the different categories of work faculty members perform, teaching, research, clinical work and service. In the Neuroscience Department, the years of abuse of the system created some peculiarities such that some associate professors, close friends of the chairman, earn higher salaries than full professors who have more longevity on the job, but are not close friends of the chairman.

[17] During 2002 academic year, the Faculty Senate of JU made several revisions and changes in the grievance process, doing away with the separate grievance committees that each school within the university had. During the ensuing process it became clear that the case of the Neuroscience Department faculty members against Simon Wall proceeded despite the fact that a grievance could not be brought against a faculty member by a group of grievants. The grievance rules, then and now, specifically state that it is enacted to allow individual faculty members to complain against another without resorting to the interference of the judicial system outside the university. Thus, the grievance process at JU prohibits the type of "class action" that was brought against Dr. Wall in 1999. Even more disturbing is the fact that Dr. Nobb claimed in his letter to Dr. Griever that he also consulted with the University Counsel's Office on the appropriateness of the grievance proceedings to continue against Dr. Wall. Either Dr. Nobb lied in his letter to Dr. Griever or the University Counsel is ignorant of the basic rules of the Blue Book, an improbable possibility. Dr. Wall suspected all along that the process is "bent" and a "class action" is not what it was meant to be, as is clear from his letter of March 28, 2000, to the grievance committee chairman, Dr. Griever. In December of 2002, the Faculty Senate approved the suggested changes and revisions of the grievance process at JU, doing away with the separate schools' grievance committees and establishing one university-wide grievance committee instead.

[18] Simon felt that the Blue Book's rules were not being followed when only two faculty members represented all fifteen who signed on the grievance document. He thought it was just fair that if he had to spend all his time in hearings, the least the other grievants can be expected is to attend the hearings, too. Moreover, in retrospect, the grievance proceedings should never have gone forward as a "class action."

¹⁹ This point goes straight to the heart of the real purpose of the grievance against Dr. Wall. Since Simon knew from his colleagues in the Neuroscience Department how the grievance was put together and who organized it, there was no question that all the grievants would never complain unless "asked nicely" by Dr. Frank I. M. Moral and his "right hand", Dr. Stewart P. Retender. Since, at the time of the filing of the grievance, Dr. Moral was still awaiting the verdict of the committee that investigated his misconduct, he knew that his signature on a grievance against Simon would be suspected of being an act of retaliation or retribution.

²⁰ This issue of ACADEME published a one-page Report entitled: On the duty of faculty members to speak out on misconduct and was approved for publication by the American Association of University Professors' Committee B on Professional Ethics, September 1998. Thus, the statement states that on occasions, when professors have reason to believe that a faculty colleague has violated standards of professional behavior, professors should take the initiative to inquire about or to protest against unethical conduct. It also stated that not speaking out may inadvertently help to sustain conditions in which misconduct is left unchecked or even condoned. The obligation to speak out is rooted in two considerations: First, in the words of the 1940 Statement of Principles of Academic Freedom and Tenure. The common good is best served when members of the academic community effectively regulate their own affairs, which they do when they act ethically themselves and also when they seek to ensure such action by others. Second, faculty members are members of a profession, and as such should guard their own standards of professional behavior. To guard is to call attention to abuses of those standards, for in speaking out professors do exercise their duty.

²¹ Dr. David S. Neaky was the candidate for a faculty position at the Neuroscience Department to whom Simon Wall communicated the fact that Frank Moral was under investigation for scientific misconduct. He was the one who contacted Moral by e-mail about Simon's communication, a contact that spurred the "class action" grievance letter.

²² Among others, Johansson wrote: There are serious problems at this University and you would be well advised to be very cautious about accepting an appointment here."

The Lawyers Are Coming, the Lawyers Are Coming

Although the grievance battle was over for all practical purposes, the handling of Simon's complaint by the American Association of Neuroscientists regarding the counterfeiting of a signature by Frank Moral was about to become more peculiar.

On August 25, 2000, Simon called Julie Swim and requested to speak at the Association's Business Meeting that would take place during the upcoming Annual Meeting. On August 26, 2000, the following letter was sent to him by the AAN:

> *Dear Dr. Wall:*
>
> *Julie Swim has made me aware of your telephone call and request to speak at the Association's Business Meeting at our Annual Meeting. If you wish to express your concern you may do so under "Other - New Business."*
>
> *Please note that the AAN is precluded from processing your allegation of misconduct based on its Responsible Conduct Guidelines. Section VI.B of the Guidelines (attached) provides that the responsibility for dealing with alleged misconduct lies with the institution at which the work was performed.[23]*
>
> *Under Section VI.E of the Guidelines, the AAN may take additional action only following finding of misconduct by your university. This was conveyed to you earlier in the letter sent to you by Dr. Edwin in March.*
>
> *If you would like to discuss your concerns, please feel free to call me at 202/555–6666.*
>
> *With kindest regards,*
>
> *Nora Burgen*
> *Executive Director*

From Ms. Burgen's letter and the promptness of her response it was clear to Simon that the AAN had already closed the book on this case and that they were feverishly attempting to extinguish any remaining smoking twig. There was a concerted effort to discourage him from further pursuing this case.

Thus, on August 27, Simon faxed the following letter to Ms. Burgen:

Dear Ms. Burgen:

Thank you for your prompt response to my inquiry regarding the Association's Business Meeting at the Annual Meeting.

While I perfectly understand your notion for precluding the AAN from processing an allegation of scientific misconduct, it is of paramount importance that such an allegation is differentiated from the allegation I brought to your attention in November 1999, and again in January 2000. My allegation is not concerned with scientific misconduct, but with a possible violation of the Association's own rules regarding sponsorship of an abstract submitted for presentation in the AAN's Annual meeting. The allegation of forgery of a signature on an abstract form of the AAN should not be categorized as a case of scientific misconduct, but rather it is an act of deceit, fraud and perjury. The AAN has possession of the documents that would prove innocence or guilt of the one accused of violating the Association's rules. It is the duty of The American Association of Neuroscientists, not anyone else to enforce its own rules if it is expected that its members follow these rules.

I would be willing to pursue my allegation through the appropriate channels of my university, given you provide me with a copy of the following documents: Original abstract forms with sponsor's signature of abstract #xxx.4 (1999), #yyy.17 (1998), and #zzz.5 (1997). Nevertheless, any action on my part should not relieve the AAN from its responsibility to process my allegation.

I will decide whether or not to express my concerns in regard to the enforcement of the Association's rules based on your response to this letter.

Sincerely yours,

Simon Wall, Ph.D.
Professor of Anesthesiology

Within three days, Simon received a letter from one, Stone P. Bensinger, from the Washington, D.C. office of O'Hare, Brystol, McConnel & Scharp, P.L.L.C., Attorneys at Law:

Dear Dr. Wall:

As legal counsel to the American Association of Neuroscientists (the Association), we have been asked to look into the allegations of scientific misconduct that you have brought up to the attention of the Association involving a research project at Jefferson University which resulted in allegedly fraudulent abstract being submitted to the Association. You have requested that the Association conduct a full investigation into your allegation. To date, there have apparently been no allegations of misconduct made to or investigations conducted by the Jefferson University.

From a review of the file that was provided to us, it appears you have brought this matter to the attention of the Association on several occasions. The Association has indicated that in order for it to proceed there must first be finding of official misconduct from the university where the research work was done. This is consistent with the Association's Guidelines for responsible Conduct Regarding Scientific Communication (Responsible Conduct Guidelines). The Association is not in a position to conduct formal investigations into scientific misconduct and appropriately leaves that to the agencies or organizations where the research work was done.

You have noted in your correspondence that you believe this is more than a case of scientific misconduct and that it involves a violation of the Associations rules on submission of abstracts. You have also stated that the Association has in its possession evidence to prove the violation of its rules. The substance of your contention, however, is still scientific misconduct and the Association's Responsible Conduct Guidelines requires a formal finding by the institution where the research was

119

performed before taking its own action. The documents that the Association has in its possession do not prove anything. The Association would have to take those documents and conduct a formal investigation to prove the member misconduct and that is precisely what the Responsible Conduct Guidelines provide is the responsibility of the institution where the research was performed.

If the Association is to be contacted by Jefferson University on this matter, the Association would be more than happy to cooperate in their investigation and to supply them with a copy of the signature in question.

If you have any questions with respect to this matter, please do not hesitate to contact me.

Sincerely yours,

Stone P. Bensinger

Simon found the claim that his university should be the one that must investigate a member of the AAN who allegedly broke the rules of this Association, outrageous. Moreover, the important point of Section VI.B of the Responsible Conduct Regarding Scientific Communication Guidelines which specifically states that **"if, after an initial inquiry, the Program Director believes that an accusation of misconduct may have merit, then the Program Director must notify the institutions at which the research was conducted,"** was never touched upon in Mr. Bensinger's letter or for that matter, in any of Ms. Burgen's letters.

The AAN had chosen to ignore and neglect its responsibility in investigating (initial inquiry) and notifying (based on merit) the institution where the alleged misconduct was committed.

Nevertheless, Simon tried once more to get the process moving and thus on September 2, 2000, he faxed Mr. Bensinger the following letter:

Dear Mr. Bensinger:

Thank you very much for your letter of August 31, 2000, explaining to me the standing of the American Association of Neuroscientists on the issue I have raised.

As I have indicated in my letter to Ms. Nora Burgen (August 27, 2000), I am willing to look into bringing my allegation to the appropriate channels at Jefferson University. However, to do so, I need copies of the original abstracts as listed in the above letter. Is there a way these can be provided to me?

Sincerely yours,

Simon Wall, Ph.D.

The next day Simon received the following response:

Dear Dr. Wall:

I have received your memo of September 2, 2000, requesting a copy of certain abstracts that have been submitted to the American Association of Neuroscientists. I have checked with the Association about their policy on release of abstracts to non-authors and discovered the abstracts and copies of the abstracts are never released except to the authors of the abstracts. As such, I am not in a position to establish a new precedent by releasing copies of abstracts to you. Consistent with the Responsible Conduct Guidelines, the Association would consider releasing the abstracts to the University as part of the University's formal investigation.

If you should have any additional questions, please do not hesitate to contact me.

Very truly yours,

Stone P. Bensinger

That ended this chapter in the tale of avoidance of responsibility and "buck passing." Simon thought how fitting it could be for the AAN to adopt as its logo an illustration of three monkeys' brains, one without the *visual cortex* (see no evil), a second without the *inferior colicullus* (hear no evil) and a third without the *olfactory bulb* (smell no evil).

Notes

[23] The title of Section VI.B is: If, after an initial inquiry, the Program Director believes that an accusation of misconduct may have merit, then the Program Director must notify the institutions at which the research was conducted. The AAN and the Program Director never conducted an initial inquiry and, even if they did, it was their duty to notify the institution. The fact that they insisted on their demand that Dr. Wall notify Jefferson University could indicate that such an inquiry did take place and misconduct was evident, however, the AAN did not wish to get involved in any proceedings.

Face to Face

To end his torturous and mentally exhausting journey, Simon was about to meet his wannabe prosecutor, judge and executioner, Dean Nobb, and soon thereafter, those who had toed the line at the American Association of Neuroscientists.

On September 3, 2000, Simon sent an e-mail message to Dr. Nobb's secretary:

Dear Ms. Shaw:

Over a year ago I tried to arrange for a meeting with Dr. Nobb, twice through you, by phone, and once by sending him a personal and confidential letter, but to no avail.

Is there a possibility for me to meet with Dr. Nobb at his convenience? It is very important that such a meeting will take place. Any date is OK with me.

I would appreciate your expedited response to my request.

Sincerely yours,

Simon Wall, Ph.D.

Simon intended to use such a meeting with the Dean to face him squarely on several specific issues regarding the Dean's refusal to meet with him earlier and, of course, the Dean's stand on the Moral & Heat's misconduct case and the grievance case against Simon.

Ms. Shaw's response was prompt:

Dr. Wall:

Will you tell me what this is concerning? Any information you can provide the Dean related to your request would be helpful, e.g., an agenda, copies of materials, or just an e-mail note of explanation.

Thank you

Cornelia Shaw
Assistant to the Dean, Medical School

Simon immediately responded to Ms. Shaw's e-mail:

Dear Ms. Shaw:

Thank you very much for your prompt response.

I would like to meet with Dr. Nobb to discuss his letter of August 26, 2000, to Dr. Griever with a copy to me. In this letter Dr. Nobb wrote that he accepts the Grievance Committee's opinion that within the narrow definition used by the Committee, this grievance is dismissed. He also accepted the Committee's finding that "Dr. Wall's actions interfering in the activities of another department were inappropriate and potentially damaging to the department." Based on this finding Dr. Nobb wrote that he "direct Dr. Wall that such inappropriate actions should cease." As of today, I have not received any directive from Dr. Nobb. Moreover, those "inappropriate" actions are not spelled out. I would like to know the exact nature of the actions that Dr. Nobb directs me to cease. I also think that it is about time that Dr. Nobb and I will meet in an effort to establish productive working relationship that will benefit the Medical School and Jefferson University. I would like to explain to Dr. Nobb the nature of my scientific work and the potential it has in helping JU to reach its goal of becoming a Research I University. My intention is to cooperate with Dr. Nobb in any way I can and, as members of the same department, to get to know him personally.

I hope that this detailed e-mail message will suffice to persuade Dr. Nobb to meet with me.

I thank you again for your help.

Sincerely yours,

Simon Wall, Ph.D.

An appointment was set for Dr. Wall with Dr. Nobb for 12 noon on October 6, 2000, on the condition that Simon's departmental chairperson, Dr. Carla L. Pool,[24] would also attend the meeting.

At 11:45 AM, October 6, 2000, Simon emerged from the elevator on the 6th floor of the Administration Building and announced his presence to the Dean's secretary. She asked him to sit in the waiting room and said that the Dean would be with him shortly.

At 12:15 PM the secretary reappeared and explained to Simon that someone was still with the Dean and apologized for the long wait. It was not until 12:30 PM that Simon was called into the Dean's office where he found Drs. Nobb and Pool sitting in the corner of the office by a small round table where they invited him to join them.

After shaking hands with both, Simon sat down and Nobb, with a faked smile on his face, said: "Well, what is it that you wanted to talk about?" Simon was a bit perturbed about waiting for over forty minutes outside the Dean's office and even more so when he found out that the reason for his long wait was Dr. Pool. She was supposed to be there anyway for the Dean's appointment.

Nobb, of course, was playing the old game of "I'd show you who's the boss here" and as part of this game he also pretended not to know what Simon wanted to talk about. Simon decided to be firm and straight to the point.

"Dr. Nobb, you have refused to see me for over a year, that is, until today. You had the opportunity to resolve the grievance case against me last year when the chair of the Grievance Committee turned the case to you, since he thought it did not fall under the Committee's jurisdiction. You decided to return the case to the Committee, ordered them to reconsider it as any other grievance case and then render a decision. Apparently, you did not like the Committee's report and their decision that the grievants did not prove their case against me. Instead of accepting the Committee's decision you asked them to reconsider the case using a wider definition of wrongdoing. When the Grievance Committee returned their report to you unchanged, you accepted it, yet, directed me to cease any inappropriate action. There are two questions I would like to ask you. One, what do you have against me? Two, what inappropriate actions you want me to cease?"

If Nobb was a bit taken aback by Simon's strong and somewhat long statement, he did not show it. He simply lied with a straight face:

"You see, Simon, I am not familiar with the details of the grievance case."

But, of course, Nobb was familiar with and interested in the case so much so that he read every word of the original grievance and the accompanying material the Grievance Committee sent to him back in December 1999. He was so familiar and interested that he decided to seek the opinion of the University Counsel's Office. Then, upon receiving the Committee's report, he was familiar enough with the case to ask the Committee to reconsider their decision.

Yet, he told Simon, while not even one muscle flinching in his face, that he was not familiar with the case. Although, Nobb never answered Simon's questions, he had a rabbit in his hat. He opened a manila folder that was lying in front of him on the desk and pulled out what appeared to be a photocopy of a document. He laid it in front of Simon and said:

"Would you tell me what is this?"

Simon looked at the photocopy in front of him and immediately recognized it as a copy of a letter of his that was published in the local newspaper's editorial pages "Readers' Opinions." The letter, entitled "'Money for Minds' Slogan Demeaning" was a response to an op-ed article in the newspaper a week earlier by the President of the University, Dr. J.V. Shepherd.

The President's article was about a new program of the Kansas government to help state universities,[25] a program that was given the title "Money for Minds."

He raised his eyes and said to Nobb:

"This is a copy of a letter of mine published last month in the Jefferson City Times."

Dr. Nobb looked at Dr. Pool, who was sitting quietly throughout, and said to Simon:

"You need not criticize the President in the newspaper! If you have complaints of any sort, just come to see me and we can discuss them."

Simon did not know whether he should laugh or simply ignore Nobb's comment. After all, he had to wait for more than a year to have

126

this appointment with the Dean and now he is being told that if he were to have a problem, the only thing he needed to do was to come straight to the dean and talk about it.

Simon decided not to respond to the dean's offer and instead simply reminded Nobb that actually his letter is full of compliments for the President and that the criticism is of the slogan. They all agree that it is time to do the job "we are all here to do" and with that the appointment was over.

Simon left the Dean's office disgusted, but not surprised. The highest-ranking administrator in the Medical School, an M.D., who has built and spent his career in academic institutions, showed no regard for academic freedom. He shamelessly signaled to Simon that criticizing anything the university's administration does is unacceptable. The Dean blatantly attempted to censor Simon's free expression of opinions and ideas where JU is concerned. Such censorship, when added to the fact that none of Simon's questions were answered, brought him to feel revulsion and frustration at his own beloved School.

Simon's direct encounter with the phenomenon of scientific misconduct and its cover-up ended with his participation at the November 2000 Business Meeting of the American Association of Neuroscientists.

When given the floor, Simon briefly described his continued disagreement with the AAN officials who refused to initiate an inquiry based on Simon's complaint of alleged misconduct.

First, the outgoing President, Dr. James F. Edwin, and immediately thereafter, the incoming one, Dr. Derrek R. Church, repeated the official line of the AAN that it is the responsibility of the university where the work was done to pursue such investigation. After the meeting, both Edwin and Church approached Simon and apologized for the fact that their hands were tied. Several others in the audience also came to talk with Simon, some of them encouraging and complimenting him for coming forward, others with advice for how to further pursue the case. Nevertheless, Simon had already made up his mind not to continue to "battle the windmills."

His last communication with any official of the American Association of Neuroscientists occurred in December 2000, when he called Ms. Burgen on the phone to ask for a copy of the minutes of the

November 2000 Business Meeting. He never received a copy of those minutes. Instead, on February 18, 2001, at 4:53 PM he received the following e-mail from Nora Burgen:

Dear Dr. Wall:

Below is a summary of the Business Meeting minutes. Please let me know if I can be of any more help.

Thank you,

Nora

Church opened the floor for discussion of any new business. Dr. Simon Wall from Jefferson University stated that last year he asked the AAN to look into a case of alleged misconduct. Edwin stated that the AAN could only respond to a request from an institution that has already looked into the problem to see if there is a possibility of misconduct. Edwin reiterated that the leadership of the AAN consulted with the Association's legal counsel on this issue. The counsel stated that the AAN is not an investigative body, and can only respond to a request from an institution that has already conducted an investigation.

Dr. Wall stated that he believed the AAN possessed the documents (abstract forms) that would demonstrate this misconduct. Edwin pointed out that a form could not be released to anyone other than the person who submitted it. He again stated that the AAN would need to be approached from the institution.

Dr. Church stated that as the new President, he and Edwin would continue to be available to Dr. Wall to continue to provide assistance within the legal bounds and protocol of the AAN, and to assist in bringing this issue to closure.

Notes

24 Pool had assumed the chairpersonship in August 2000. An old friend of Dr. Nobb, she applied for the position after he had nominated her. In addition, there

128

were several other outstanding candidates who applied for the position vacated by Dr. Barry A. L. Truist after 20 years at the helm of the department. Among the candidates there was a graduate of the Medical School at JU, Dr. Joel C. Newberg, who had an excellent reputation both as an anesthesiologist and as a researcher at Stanford University. He was unanimously selected by the search committee as its top candidate and was offered the job. Dr. Newberg presented a list of demands to be met by the Medical School for him to accept the position. Dr. Nobb rejected those demands as unacceptable. Other candidates who were interviewed all withdrew their candidacy except Dr. Pool. As the sole candidate for the job, the faculty members had to vote her up or down. Over 80% of the voting faculty members rejected her candidacy. When Dr. Nobb was given the official tally of the vote he immediately summoned two of his associates who called for a special faculty meeting of the Anesthesiology Department for the day after the vote. At the meeting, Associate Dean for Faculty Affairs, Dr. Lola I. Serve, announced that the vote on Dr. Pool's candidacy was null and void since two part-time faculty members who were ineligible to vote, voted anyway. Dr. Serve also made it clear to everyone present that the Dean would seriously consider aborting his efforts to achieve re-accreditation of the residency program in Anesthesiology, which was put on probation the year before and annul altogether the Department as an independent entity, making it part of the Surgery Department, unless the vote in favor of Dr. Pool was achieved. In the revote that took place that very day, 80% of the faculty members voted for Dr. Pool as the new chair of the Anesthesiology Department.

[25]   This is the full text of Dr. Simon Wall's letter published in the Jefferson City Times: "Money for Minds Slogan 'Demeaning'". In a Sept. 1 letter, Dr. James V. Shepherd, the president of Jefferson University, eloquently explained Gov. Soul Satton's program named "Money for Minds" and its vision. Shepherd's letter attempted to justify the use of funds from this program for hiring an ex-government employee for a teaching and administrative position at the MacCauly Center for Political Leadership. Shepherd's contributions to Jefferson University are indisputable. His ability to present the university's needs and vision both to the legislature and the community is unmatched. Yet, despite the riches that have befallen our institution, existing faculty members, who have served with excellence, are not sharing in these riches. No one within the university's community should question the importance of investing 3% of $70 million in an undergraduate program. What one should question is, why aren't similar investments being made in existing faculty members whose minds are as good as the minds of those being recruited from other universities? I find the slogan "Money for Minds" demeaning and demoralizing. Although some may read it differently, one cannot avoid the slogan's connotation that no minds are to be found on the campus of Jefferson University, and thus, one must look for minds somewhere else. Moreover, this slogan may represent the excellent researchers being recruited for lucrative positions as greedy scholars who sell their minds to the highest bidder. I doubt the slogan "Money for Minds" is the creation of an educator. More likely, it is the invention of an administrator or a legislator. Let's change it to fit better our university's mission, something like "Initiative for Prominence in Research and Teaching" or "Campaign for

Excellence in Research and Learning" or any other slogan as long as the mighty Dollar is not what we are all about."

Epilogue

The roller coaster journey of Dr. Simon Wall that began in May 1998, ended 30 months later without making much difference in a system that had chosen to discard some of the most paramount principles of ethical scientific research, while adopting some of the rules that govern the stock market. Simon also found out that, in today's climate, there is more in common between science and religion where cover-up of wrongdoing is concerned.

Almost four years have passed since Simon filed away the hundreds of documents he collected throughout this ordeal, along with the emotions that at one time drove him to visit the doctor after a three months bout with high blood pressure.

Although he committed himself completely to his research endeavors and has seen much success both in prolific publication of scientific papers and in attracting research funds, his experience as a whistleblower has made a profound change in the way he looks at science and its administration.

There are the daily reminders, mainly as momentary encounters with one or another of those who ganged up on him in the grievance case, as he walks through the halls and yards of the campus. The administration, in contrast, hasn't given-up on retaliating against him. Thus, attempts to cut his research space, the most effective tool the administration still has to discipline the nonconformists, are continuing.

Simon was the first one in the Medical School with whom the administration attempted to apply a new policy for allocation of research space according to which a faculty member who does research must garner $200 worth of federal grant funds for every one square foot of research space per year. Thus, for a moderate research space of 1000 square feet, said faculty member must raise a minimum of $200,000 a year in federal financial support. While this standard works for universities such as Stanford, Princeton, Duke, UCLA, and others, Jefferson University still has a long way to go before joining the ranks of those giants. Less than 20% of all research faculty members at JU could boast their ability to pay such high rate of "rent" for research space in this obscure university somewhere in the Midwest.

Hence, although thriving to achieve such a high standard is commendable, using it as a tool of retaliation against whistleblowers assures that this standard is never to be achieved. Recently, Simon also encountered difficulties in the process of submission of applications for research grants. There were ample signs and hints that certain administrators in the Office of Grants Management are slowing down the processing of his applications. In one particular case, the dean held one of Simon's applications for almost four months without signing on it, hoping to prevent the funding of this grant. The excuse given to Simon was that the grant forms were lost in the shuffle.

Naturally, with this bitter experience under his belt, Simon frequently wonders whether or not he would blow the whistle again. And if he would, what would he do differently? What advice should he give to others would-be whistleblowers?

Obviously, Simon's will to bring about a change for the better is still there, otherwise this book would have not been written. Changes must take place both at the level of self-policing by scientists for ethical conduct of research and at the level of enforcement by the academicians themselves and their administrators. On both levels, the situation in the academia today is very similar to the one in the Catholic Church. In both institutions wrongdoing and cover-up by their administrations have occurred.

However, while the Church seems to have reached the point where the cover-up of wrongdoing is a known fact and, thus, no longer successful, academic institutions are not there, yet. Sooner or later, however, universities will learn that a good name is worth much more than all the money saved or gained in covering up misconduct.

Yes, money and power are at the root of the problem and are the main impetus for wrongdoers and their protectors to engage in these activities.

One need not be a psychologist to realize that a scientist, especially at the rank of full professor, who engages in scientific misconduct, must have done it before. While Simon Wall had no first hand knowledge of any previous scientific misconduct committed by Frank Moral, certain repetitive behavioral traits and tactics he had applied in the case of Dr. Lidia Quarry were brought up against him during the hearings leading to her lawsuit.

Thus, several past colleagues of Dr. Moral gave depositions in which they described how he forced them out of their job in situations similar to that of Dr. Quarry. Attempts to understand the personality of the unethical scientist have been made[26] where it was suggested: *"when a person sees ego-inflation, monetary gain, power, or prestige the criterion for success, engaging in fraudulent behavior will cause minimal dissonance arousal."*

It is clear that Dr. Frank I. M. Moral's engagement in fraudulent behavior did not appear to cause him any dissonance arousal. His first response to the exposure of his plagiarism was an actual admission that he had copied his own student's thesis in his grant proposal. He had justified his actions by claiming that he would have cited the thesis if not for the fact that its availability is extremely limited.

Moral was counting on the acceptance of such a ridiculous excuse by the administration, although, he should know that scientists would feel intellectually insulted by it. However, at the time of his making this excuse, Moral could not afford to throw the blame on his devoted assistant, Wendy S. Capegoat, since she was, at the time, still in control of most of her faculties.

As the investigation dragged on and as it became clear to Frank Moral that the scandal would not disappear, he had to come up with a better escape plan. The deterioration of Wendy Capegoat's health, the loss of most of her cognitive functions and the unavoidable prognosis of her looming death, offered an opportunity to Frank I. M. Moral that did not exist earlier. Hence, in his interview with *the Jefferson City Times'* reporter Frank had already used Wendy as his scapegoat and during his testimony to the IARS committee he openly blamed her of plagiarism.

The most egregious act of Dr. Frank I. M. Moral occurred when he picked up his pen and signed Wendy S. Capegoat's name on one of the abstract forms submitted to the 1999 Annual Meeting of the American Association of Neuroscientists. He blamed his dying assistant for his scientific misconduct, while at the same time he forged her signature on an official document that benefited him. This is the best example of a fraudulent activity that caused minimal dissonance arousal in Frank I. M. Moral.

Therefore, to counter the diminished dissonance arousal in unethical scientists and those who engage in protecting them, individuals and institutions that are involved in cover-up of cases of scientific misconduct should be considered as guilty as the scientists who commit them. It is also important to recognize and classify acts of retaliation and retributions against whistleblowers as inseparable part of the act of cover-up.

As to Dr. Christian C. Heat, in retrospect, Simon did have first hand knowledge of what could amount to an earlier scientific misconduct on Heat's part.

As a clinician, Heat had very little interest in research, especially in laboratory research. However, as a medical school faculty member, who had been involved in the teaching of residents, promotion through the academic ranks meant that he had to publish his research work in peer-reviewed journals. In the mid-1980s, when the time for his promotion to the rank of professor approached, his boss, Dr. H. L. Powerhouse, told Heat that his list of publications must be boosted in order for the promotion application to sail through the several committees and administrators responsible for its approval.

Then Heat made a great effort to establish collaborations with several basic scientists hoping to increase the number of his peer-reviewed publications. Simon was one of those scientists who were approached by Heat.

Simon made it very clear to the neurologist that the only way they could work together was for Heat to personally be involved in the execution of the experiments and the writing of any manuscript that would result from these experiments.

With this understanding, Heat spent a great deal of time in Simon's laboratory and had hand-on experience with the research set-up. He worked closely with Simon's technician on a project that Heat himself suggested and the results quickly accumulated to a point where there was enough to generate at least one publication. Soon thereafter, Heat devoted himself to the writing of the manuscript.

On May 6, 1988, Simon received, via the internal university mail service, a copy of a manuscript submitted for publication to the clinical journal *Surgical Neurology* by Dr. Heat. Simon read it and the next day sent Dr. Heat a letter stating a) that the manuscript listed Simon's name as a co-author, b) that Simon was not given an opportunity to read and approve it before its submission, and c) that the manuscript in its present form could not meet Simon's approval. Simon's letter also listed numerous errors, inconsistencies and outright false statements that were included in the manuscript. No response from Heat was received to that letter.

On June 1, 1988, Simon sent the following letter to the Editor of *Surgical Neurology*:

Dear Dr. Hague:

Four weeks ago a manuscript by C.C. Heat et al., was submitted for publication in your journal.

As a co-author of this manuscript I was surprised to find out that it was sent out without my having the opportunity to see it before submission.

I am enclosing a copy of a letter I sent to Dr. Heat on May 7, 1988, concerning this matter.

Since Dr. Heat, as of today, has not responded to that letter, I have decided to withdraw my name from the above manuscript.

Sincerely yours,

Simon Wall, Ph.D.
Associate Professor of Anesthesiology

On June 4, 1988, Dr. Simon Wall received the following letter from the Editor-in-Chief of the journal:

Dear Dr. Wall:

Your paper (manuscript #xxx-88) was received and we have begun to circulate it among our peer-review editors. We will certainly adhere to your interest in this matter and not publish it or accept it for publication without consultation with you and whatever corrections you see are fit. We will certainly be glad to remove your name from the publication in the event it is accepted for publication.

Sincerely yours,

A. Hague, M.D.

On June 19, 1988, Dr. Simon Wall received the following short letter from the Editor-in-Chief:

Dear Dr. Wall:

Our peer review editors believe this paper (manuscript #xxx-88), on which you were listed as a coauthor, should be published in Surgical Neurology. If you want us to remove your name from the list of authors, I shall be glad to do so.

Sincerely yours,

A. Hague, M.D.

Simon found this response unbelievable, considering the fact that the editor had received a full and long list of inaccuracies, errors and outright false statements that were included in the manuscript submitted by Dr. Heat.

One of the most egregious unethical acts of Dr. Heat was the inclusion in the paper of a statement that claimed that a specific analysis was performed and that the results of that analysis were as expected. Moreover, the name of the scientist who supposedly performed this analysis was added to the list of authors. Since Simon had first hand knowledge and awareness of all the experiments performed in the study, he knew that such an analysis was never performed and this ghost co-author had never received any material from Simon's lab to perform the mentioned analysis.

On June 25, 1988, Simon sent the following letter to Dr. Hague, the Editor-in-Chief of Surgical Neurology.

Dear Dr. Hague:

Thank you for your letter of June 19, 1988. Since I, along with my technician were the ones who performed all the experiments included in this manuscript with Dr. Heat, but were not consulted during its writing, I find it unacceptable for publication in its present form. The inaccuracies and omissions

137

found in the manuscript do not allow me to lend my name to this product. Unfortunately, you did not mention in your letter whether or not the corrections I requested are now included in the published version. Unless those corrections are included, I will have no choice but to ask you to remove my name from the list of authors on this manuscript.

Sincerely yours,

Simon Wall, Ph.D.
Associate Professor of Anesthesiology

On July 1, 1988, Simon received the following letter From Dr. Hague:

Dear Dr. Wall:

At your request, we will leave your name off of the manuscript, and all the corrections that you have suggested will be made. We thank you for your correspondence.

Sincerely yours,

A. Hague, M.D.

This letter was somewhat confusing, since it stated that the corrections Simon suggested would be incorporated yet, his name would be removed from the manuscript. Nevertheless, Simon found great relief not to be associated with a peer-reviewed paper written by an author who had no qualms about fabricating experimental results.

Notwithstanding, for reasons unbeknown to Simon, as of today, 16 years later, that manuscript still awaits publication. It is possible that Dr. Hague had realized, after all, the risk his journal would take in publishing a manuscript that included fabricated data.

Thus, this almost forgotten incidence from the 1980s could indicate that Heat, who was exonerated from any wrongdoing in the plagiarism case with Dr. I. M. Moral, is a scientist of the type with a minimal dissonance arousal who would not hesitate to commit a scientific misconduct if and when the personal benefit from such act would be worth the risk.

The events described in this book expose, most likely for the first time, the paramount role that a university administration played in covering up scientific misconduct committed by two of its leading academicians.

One must realize that attempts at covering up wrongdoing are routine occurrences in almost every walk of life. Families would regularly cover-up the misdeeds of one of their members if and when exposure of the misdeeds would blemish the family's reputation. Organizations and their bosses would circle the wagons to protect themselves from exposure of unlawful activities that could affect the bottom line on the balance sheet. Politicians and their assistants would engage in cover-up of misdeeds that could hurt reelection chances. And, of course, the Mafia has its own special ways to cover-up their illegal deals.

The will to preserve a good, intact and unblemished image of the individual, the family, the organization or the community is stronger in most cases than the will to reform, correct or expose the individual(s) who commit the misdeeds.

Consequently, once the steps toward cover-up ensue, they must go hand-in-hand with attempts to muffle those who may continue to impose risk of exposure of the misdeeds, namely, the whistleblowers. Hence, as has been mentioned above, attempts at retaliation and retribution against whistleblowers are inseparable from the cover-up attempts.

However, unlike any other community, the scientific community cannot afford to circle the wagons around its unethical few. And, although we are being told that the scientific process, sooner or later, would extract the fraudulent science, since the scientific method is self-correcting, the damage that fraud in science could cause to the general public may be beyond measurement. That is because science is a global enterprise that could, potentially, affect every human being and other living organisms on the face of the earth and beyond.

As for the whistleblower, he/she always stands alone, isolated and vulnerable, but not necessarily because his/her colleagues side with the wrongdoer. In most cases, fear of retribution from those who are in charge, CEOs, bishops, deans or other high-ranking administrators keeps the whistleblower's colleagues silent. Nevertheless, there are always those who will enthusiastically participate in the persecution of the whistleblower for potential personal gains in the future. And these gains are almost always monetary.

Those who are directly or indirectly involved in covering up wrongdoing of others are rarely, if ever, held responsible for their actions. They are usually perceived as the defenders of the institution in which the misconduct was committed and, thus, are being forgiven, and frequently are rewarded by the administration for defending the wrongdoers. After all, the defenders exhibit loyalty and communal sense, two traits that we all admire.

Only when the punishment for covering up misconduct offsets the gains perpetrators of misconduct and their defenders receive from their acts, may we have a chance to win the battle against the crime of scientific misconduct.

A system that would better protect the whistleblower and maybe even reward him/her for exposing misconduct must be put in place. We must encourage whistle blowing and offer any assistance and support to those who are willing to stand guard against those who recklessly and selfishly betray the trust the general public has in science and scientists.

These days one can find a great deal of information about both scientific misconduct and whistle blowing. Books, websites, reports, opinions, rules, even notices by the National Institutes of Health (NIH) about findings of scientific misconduct, all are out there for the interested. Most of the information is available on the internet and scientists and students of science are all advised to search for resources on these topics.

The majority of this material accumulated after 1998, the same year Simon Wall began his journey into the dark side of science. If any, this material should make us all more educated about the topic of scientific misconduct and should better prepare would-be whistleblowers for their thankless task.

Notes

26 Miller, D.J. Personality factors in scientific fraud and misconduct, in *Research Fraud in the Behavioral and Biomedical Sciences* (Miller, D.J. and Hersen, M., Eds) John Wiley & Sons, New York, pp. 125–139, 1992.

Extra!! Extra!!

Just as things seemed to settle down, the unexpected happened. In January of 2003, Dr. Shepherd accepted the Presidential position at Texas University (TU), a 52,000-student institution. His salary was reported to be one of the highest in the nation among public university presidents. But only 10 months later, on October 8, 2003, Dr. Shepherd presented his resignation to the Governor of Texas. This resignation followed scrutiny by the media of his lavish spending on travel, entertainment and on his university-provided mansion and the heavy use of the university airplane.

Many of his business trips on the TU plane were to Little Rock, Arkansas, where his colleague and friend, the ex-provost of JU, Caroline X. Pretty, had assumed the position of president of Arkansas University. Of the 25 flights Dr. Shepherd took during his short stay at TU on the university airplane, nine were to Little Rock.

Several damaging details about the ex-president of JU came out following an investigation by a local TV station in San Antonio and an audit by the state of Texas of Dr. Shepherd's expenses as the president of TU.

Thus, it was revealed that Shepherd received a $10,000 gift from Mitsubishi of Japan in 1996, which he described as "congratulatory gift" after signing a training contract with the automaker on behalf of Eastern Maine State University (EMSU) while President there. The acceptance of the gift violated state ethics laws. Shortly after he assumed his position at JU, Shepherd, an unmarried divorcee, applied for a marriage license with the nanny of his children, a former EMSU student from China without actual plans to wed her, but to help her with visa problems. Despite hundreds of thousands of dollars spent for remodeling the President's mansion at TU just prior to Dr. Shepherd's acceptance of the presidential position, upon his arrival, he ordered additional renovations at a cost of several hundred thousand dollars more. Among the renovations were a $10,000 grill and $60,000 for an audio and telephone system. This type of splurging by Shepherd exemplified how similar the life style of an American public university CEO (President) to that of an American corporation CEO has become.

As a result of the information that became available following the investigation and the audit in Texas, both JU and EMSU decided to audit all Shepherd's credit card receipts and travel and entertainment expenses while he was the president at these institutions.

The revelations about the lavish life style and big spending of public funds, at times of great constraints on public university funding, by Dr. Shepherd at EMSU, JU and TU, and the increase in the number of scientific misconduct cases such as the one committed by Drs. Moral and Heat at JU, illustrate the risks that academic institutions are taking these days in their efforts to garner additional funds beyond the allocated state budget. In most universities today the productivity of a scientist is measured not by the quality of his/her science, but by the number of dollars he/she has amassed from extramural sources.

Moreover, since the survival of modern university research scientists depends entirely on their ability to attract research dollars, the temptation by some to cut corners, to cheat, or to resort to unethical behavior is growing. The administrations of public universities, with the full support of their boards of trustees, are searching for the best fund-raiser as university presidents and are willing to pay outrageously high salaries and bonuses to the right candidates. With this strong emphasis on money, it is not surprising that the number of misconduct cases by both scientists and top administrators is on the rise.

If we are to preserve and protect our academic institutions from the scourge of big money and human weaknesses, we must find a way to uncover the corrupt ones and prohibit their participation in the normal ethical and honest conduct of science.